THE WIND BLOWS
AWAY OUR WORDS

DORIS LESSING

THE WIND BLOWS AWAY OUR WORDS

and Other Documents Relating to the Afghan Resistance

Vintage Books
A Division of Random House
New York

Library of Congress Cataloging-in-Publication Data
Lessing, Doris May, 1919—
The wind blows away our words.
1. Afghanistan—History—Soviet occupation,
1979—   . Title.
DS371.2.L47 1987   958'.1044   87-40009
ISBN 0-394-75504-9

ACKNOWLEDGMENTS

'Only my own kind will kill me'
from a poem by Osip Mandlestam,
Selected Poems, Penguin Modern European Poets.
The Chronology of the Modern World
1763–1965, Penguin.

Manufactured in the United States of America
10 9 8 7 6 5 4 3 2 1

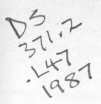
To the gallant people of
Afghanistan

We cry to you for help, but the wind blows
away our words.

Muhjahid Commander
Peshawar, 1986

CONTENTS

PART ONE

*Her Long Hair
Streaming Loose*

The legend goes like this. Apollo, with time on his hands, turned his attention to those little creatures on earth, all busily pursuing their destinies, as we have to do. Noticing Cassandra, a toothsome girl, he said: 'Well, how about a quickie then? You won't lose by it – I'll give you the power of prophecy.' 'I don't mind if I do,' said she, but cheated, once she knew she could foretell the future. Apollo was angry. He was revengeful, too: then an admired quality. 'Let's have a kiss at least,' said he, and she agreed. During this embrace he took away half of his gift: she would be able to prophesy, but no one would believe her. Some versions say that Apollo breathed into her mouth; others, equally squeamish, that he 'took in her breath'. What really happened, it seems, was that he spat into her mouth – like a serpent. Snakes and the origins of Cassandra intertwine. She and her twin brother were left by their parents, who were drunk and forgetful after a binge, in a shrine. When this remorseful pair returned to collect their infants, 'their ears were being licked by the sacred serpents of the shrine'. This is one version of how Cassandra came by her prophesying.

Cassandra, daughter of Priam, who was King of Troy, warned, 'her hair streaming loose' of the forthcoming disastrous war, but no one took any notice. Various ill-considered acts on the part of Troy contributed to the start of this war; the beautiful Helen was not entirely to blame. Everyone on both sides, in fact, went on behaving – as it seems they had to – so as to make this war inevitable. It duly began. Then it went on.

There was a lot of what we would call collaboration. Cassandra herself, daughter of Troy's king, had two children by Agamemnon, king of the attacking forces. Helen. . .well now, Helen is an interesting case. In shortened versions of the tale, or those done for children, she is passive, passed from hand to hand, diced for, coveted, squabbled over, never blamed for anything; like a doll, or a smiling statue imbued with sanctity. She was divine, being the daughter of Zeus. Was she beautiful because she was divine, or divine because she was beautiful? All of Troy, it was said, was in love with her: this sounds like the Virgin Mary in certain countries. But it is more fascinating to believe her irresistibly beautiful.

And she was certainly not passive.

She and Cassandra often reflect different facets of a quality: one of the epithets or praise-names used for Cassandra was: She who entangles men.

Cassandra was shipped back to Mycenae with the war booty, as Agamemnon's property, and Clytaemnestra, jealous of her, had her put to death. Cassandra knew of the plot to kill her and Agamemnon: she 'smelled blood'. Mind you, even without the smell of blood it would not have been all that difficult to foresee that her lover's wife was likely to be upset. She refused to enter the chamber where Agamemnon, her lover, her enemy, the father of her two children, was being slaughtered. But if she had not then herself been killed, she would of course have gone on, in moments when she was distraught, her hair streaming loose, making intelligent predictions. And no one would have taken a blind bit of notice.

14

Well, now. We have changed, and so has our view of the Gods. (Our view of the Gods at any given time could almost be regarded as a litmus paper, or geiger counter – a measure of our development, or stage, in evolution.) They are no longer vengeful, or moody, or capricious triflers with human destiny, mating on a whim with this or that pretty mortal, given to horse-play and embarrassing practical jokes. We may envisage them brooding painfully on human folly, wondering when, if ever, their protégés will learn some sense. 'If only they could acquire just a little of Our *nous*! Surely it is time they absorbed Our foresight, farsightedness, ability to see what is likely to result from what they do, or think? We are always doing what We can, to prevent this or that stupidity – though of course they seldom recognize Our intervention in their affairs, they are so conceited. We put ideas into their heads which they fondly believe are their own. . .yes, We do as much as they will allow Us to do. And there are always those few, precious people who try to approach Us, become Us, absorb Our wisdom – and through them we are able to influence human destiny a little. But they do have to learn the first rule, which is, when to speak and when to keep silent. The trouble is that so many given even a taste of Us, lose their heads and think that that is what it is all about: letting down their hair and generally carrying on. . .they don't want to go through the long boring process of fitting themselves to be fit for conversations with Us – not at all, they rush about, babbling about Insights and Intuition, full of self-importance, purveying bits of unsuitable and out-of-context information, in and out of season. . .saints, prophets, prophetesses, martyrs. . . '

What I would like to know is, who, apart from

Cassandra in Priam's palace was talking about the imminent war? Only Cassandra? – of course not. No, there were probably quite a few, a sizable minority, for whom the name 'Cassandra' is shorthand. She was a princess, distraught, with streaming locks, shouting 'Woe, Woe!' – but in the kitchens old wives who had seen it all before muttered and gloomed, and a beggar who had been a soldier crippled in an earlier war haunted the battlements of Troy, grabbing by the arm everybody who passed. 'This war will be a calamity for us all!' he shouted, (for he was a bit deaf from a spear wound), 'a calamity for the Greeks as well as for us!' But he was touched in the wits, poor old thing, and everyone knew Cassandra was too highstrung for her good.

Once upon a time, there were the special, talented-for-prophecy individuals. Then, a few people in every palace, settlement, farmstead. But now, a multitude. These days Cassandra is not a divinely inspired sybil, or old women weeping disregarded in corners, or old soldiers who lost everything in a war. Cassandra is a shout of warning coming from everywhere, particularly from scientists whose function it is to know what is likely to happen, from people everywhere who concern themselves with public affairs, anyone who thinks at all. You could say the whole world has become Cassandra, since there can be no one left who does not see disasters ahead. They are all of them preventable, preventable, that is, if we were in fact in charge of our destinies, as we imagine we are; or as it could be supposed we think we are, judging by how we talk.

We all know, or talk as if we know, that we should not destroy the world's rain forests, cut down forests on mountainsides where the run-off of water can wash precious

16

topsoil into the oceans, allow deserts to spread (they have been spreading for centuries, millenia). We should not put poisons into oceans, or let loose radioactivity that makes regions of our world uninhabitable. We should not manufacture nuclear weapons, because we are a careless, unreliable breed. We should not go to war at all, there are more sensible ways of settling differences. We should not. . . should not. . .should not. . . And we should, should, should. . . .

I sat on a headland over Sydney and watched the sky over the hinterland darken, as with a cloud of locusts. I thought I was seeing locusts, having often watched, when young, this low dark streak on the horizon growing tall and thick until half the sky is covered, then all the sky – but no, it was dust, it was the soil from thousands of farms being driven by the wind over Sydney to be dumped into the sea, millions of tons of topsoil, gone forever, because the trees are being cut. Australia has cut down a third of its trees, while knowing, this it goes without saying, that to do it causes deserts.

This year we have seen the accidents at Chernobyl, and the poisoning of the Rhine by Switzerland; both catastrophes of the kind Cassandra knew would happen, even if the experts didn't. And will happen again. And again.

Recently, Paul Erlich (one of the nuclear winter warners) said that the real question we (humanity) should put to ourselves is, 'why do we go on doing things that we all know will harm us, perhaps irretrievably? *What is the matter with us all?*' Of course there have been others who have asked, What is the matter with us? Koestler among them.

It is amusing to imagine (because the thing is so un-

17

likely) a secret conference called by the nations, who have agreed to set aside all the slogans and battle cries and the circling for better positions just for the duration of the conference, which will discuss: 'What is the matter with us, what is wrong with mankind, that we can't listen to Cassandra? It is as if the world, as if we, were being dragged along by some undertow of stupidity too powerful to resist, and all the sharp, frantic, desperate cries of warning are like gulls glinting as they wheel over the scene, and then dip and vanish, screaming, *If you do this, then that must follow*— Surely there must be something we can all do, together; perhaps we can learn to listen. . . '

Probably when Cassandra was murdered outside the great halls of Agamemnon's palace, it was not only because she was the king's fancy woman, but because everyone knew she would go on prophesying doom, and doom, and they did not want to listen. They knew they could not help themselves.

But why can we not help ourselves?

We do not know.

Meanwhile there are hints and signposts along the way, reflecting our attitudes, our propensities.

Velikovsky said, when asked how could it be that all the dreadful catastrophes he described as being the foundation of our history are not remembered at all, or, if remembered, only as legends or myths, 'We forget catastrophes'. We cannot endure the memory of the worst that has happened – planets or meteors colliding with us, sudden shifts of climate, the sea level suddenly rising and drowning whole cities, civilizations. . . '

'Now come on, then,' I remember thinking, reading Velikovsky. 'We forget, do we? Yet our history books are chronicles of disaster – wars, famines, epidemics. Not only do we remember what has happened but often there is a note of satisfied solemnity in our remembering, of relish, a veritable organ note of pleasurable commemoration. You say we forget? What proof have you?'

Well then, let us consider this. The First World War's dead numbered four million. This was modest compared to the horrors that were to follow, and very soon. The seven to nine million of Stalin's forced collectivization of Russian peasants. The twenty million (or so) of Stalin's murders in the Gulags. The twenty million (or so) of the Great Leap Forward. The sixty million (or so) of the Cultural Revolution. But these were deliberate murders, policies of murder, planned and carried out. The four million of the First World War were not planned, were not meant, they happened. At the time it was terrible, impossible, dreadful – all Europe was afflicted by the numbers of the dead, perhaps sensing that they marked the beginning of our decline. The possibility of man-made disasters was being recognized, and with such unease and foreboding. Yet as that war ended, with its four million dead, there began a much greater calamity, the flu epidemic, which ravaged the whole world and killed twenty-nine million people. The years 1918, 1919, 1920 were horrible because of this great epidemic, quite apart from the refugees, the cripples, the devastation, the poverty made by the war. People were dying. They died in millions, many more than the four million which we have all been remembering ever since. No one knew why there was this great influenza epidemic. There was also a sleeping sickness epidemic, equally mysterious, though far fewer people died. (The memory of this epidemic, long after everyone had

forgotten about it, was revived in Dr Oliver Sacks' book
Awakenings, about people who had lived on, and on,
survivors, for several decades.) The First World War is
always being remembered, discussed, analysed. Histories
are written, heroes celebrated, we stand to attention once a
year and mourn. But the Great Influenza Epidemic that
killed more than seven times as many people is seldom
mentioned.

In *The Chronology of the Modern World* (Penguin), the
entry for 1918 reads, 'Influenza epidemic (May, June, and
October)'. The entry for 1919, 'Severe influenza epidemic, (March)'. Some person leafing through this reference book curious to get some idea of the progress of
human affairs need hardly linger over either entry. We
have influenza epidemics every year. We even have
'severe' flu epidemics. We might see a headline, 'Severe
flu epidemic in the Midlands, 79 people dead'. But
twenty-nine million people? You would never guess it,
from this, or from some other reference books.

Recently a talented young man made a film about the
year 1919, and asked me to see it. I asked, at once, 'You
mean, it is about the big flu epidemic?' 'What flu epidemic?' he asked. He had never heard of it. Highly educated people have never heard about that three-year-long
affliction, about which even now you may hear ancient
survivors talk with the stunned look that goes with certain
disasters that seemed to have no cause, could not be prevented, were not foreseen – and were quickly forgotten,
seeming to fade from the public mind, or memory.

We should be asking, perhaps, '*Why* have we forgotten
this terrible calamity?' 'What other calamities have we all
chosen to forget?' 'What is it about certain types of disaster
that numbs the human mind?'

You can read histories of Napoleon's retreat from Moscow, and not find it said that most of the troops died from typhus, dysentery, cholera. Generals Snow and Ice are plentifully commemorated. In war after war, the deciding forces were typhus, dysentery, cholera, even the Black Death. But often the histories hardly mention them.

Is is that there are kinds of calamity our minds are equipped to deal with, but others not? Are we able to remember what we feel responsible for, like war? Does this mean that, as we learn to link causes to effects, we will remember more and more?

Cassandra could not have warned, could not warn now, about the influenza epidemic, saying 'If you are stupid enough to have wars, then epidemics will follow.' Influenza and sleeping sickness followed the First World War, but there were no world epidemics after the Second World War, the Korean War, Vietnam, Cambodia – or any of the smaller wars.

I have heard old people say, remembering The Spanish Lady (the people's name for the flu epidemic – perhaps it took out the hurt to evoke something like a flamenco dancer in black lace flounces), 'God was punishing us for the wickedness of the war.' But God sometimes punishes, and sometimes not.

We cannot forecast epidemics – but some catastrophes lie certainly ahead of us.

We have only recently become prepared to talk about the rising and falling of the world's sea level, which in the past, each time it has happened, has taken everyone by surprise. And we will be taken by surprise again, since it seems we have learned nothing.

Try saying: 'We are due for another Ice Age: the scientists say that it can begin next week, or in a thousand years'

21

time. Actually, (they say) we are overdue for an Ice Age. All of history, the tales we tell each other, from Egypt to Babylonia, from China to the great civilizations that once flourished in the islands off the shores of Northern Europe, all, all of it, has happened in the little, short, warm space between two violent onslaughts of ice that covered most of Europe, that altered the rest of the world's climate, that changed the whole world. When this happens again we shall be helpless against it. How can we even run away to warmer parts of the world already over-burdened with people who will be struggling with the difficulties of adaptations to new climatic conditions? No, we shall die, almost certainly. The Ice will cover our cities, our achievements, our civilizations, our gardens and our forests, our fields and our orchards, will cover us. . . Who knows in what forms the civilizations will survive that do survive, and how life will return, when the Ice retreats again, and uncovers the tundras and permafrosts of Europe. . . '

Well – just try saying: 'We are due for another Ice Age!' It is as if people do not hear what you say. When the scientists say it, the reaction is not far off embarrassment, as if at bad taste, or some kind of wilful teasing.

In the story of Cassandra there are places where it looks as if people did not want to know the truth: as if (so it is sometimes put) 'The Gods blinded them to the truth'.

There is that curious scene in the great hall of Priam's palace. The Wooden Horse stands there, having been dragged in after much argument through the city gates – which had to be widened to let it go through. There it is. The sounds of clashing armour can be heard from inside. Cassandra, not surprisingly, is crying, 'Woe! There are

22

armed men inside.' But the optimists are prevailing. 'Those aren't really the sounds of armed men,' we may imagine them reasonably and smilingly argue. 'Or if so, then they probably mean us well. It is a mistake always to see events as threatening.' Meanwhile, something else was going on. Cassandra was not alone there by the Horse. Helen was with her. Helen was not a prophetess or a sybil, but she knew the Greeks were inside the horse, because she could hear them. She was amusing herself by strolling round the outside of the Horse and banging on its sides, and calling out the names of the men within, in the voices of their wives. What has this glimpse of Helen to do with the long-suffering beauty of the legend? She was accompanied by her then husband Deiphobus, a shadowy character of whom one is tempted to imagine that he was married off to Helen in an attempt to make an honest woman of her. Remember that she had been married to Achilles, Theseus, Menelaus, Paris (whatever the word 'married' meant then). All Troy was in love with her, and the greybeards trembled when they saw her walking veiled on the battlements.

They consulted, and appointed one of them to go to her and say: 'Now look at it from our point of view. It is a question of Public Order. Just get a wedding ring on to your finger.' He spoke in the rough, angry, depressed voice that men use when attracted to a woman but wish they were not, and Helen laughed and said, 'Just as you like.'

Just after the Wooden Horse episode, she would be putting a light in the window to guide in those Greeks who were not already in the great hall ready to jump out and kill her friends, lovers, hosts, with whom she had obviously been amicably living for years. Odysseus and Menelaus killed Deiphobus, her loving husband, and then she went off to Egypt where she lived with Menelaus.

The Gods were certainly blinding men to the truth, during the episode of the Wooden Horse. For some dark reasons of their own.

Or was it that enough people inside Troy disliked life there so much, or were exhausted enough by the tensions of waiting (a war is always a question of waiting, waiting, waiting for disaster) that they simply wanted an end to it all? An end at any cost.

Perhaps a lot of them thought the whole business was simply ridiculous anyway. What was everyone fighting about? If Greece was so horrible, what was Cassandra doing having two children by its king, children who might reasonably be expected to become part of a ruling class which would govern both states, and at last put an end to the fighting?

Helen's children? Did she have them? Surely she did. She was the type who does. Divine she might have been, but in her earthly aspect she was a famous healer. I imagine a practical, sensible, healthy woman, surrounded by children and animals, standing in her kitchen garden or in her kitchen directing the maids who are distilling potions and elixirs. They are all laughing and telling jokes that men are not meant to overhear.

Or imagine her, with Cassandra, on the windy battlements. . .the Wooden Horse is still looming there in the great hall. The men inside it will shortly jump out. Helen has pulled Cassandra out of the hall and up to the top of the castle, because she thinks some fresh air will do the poor distraught creature some good.

24

Cassandra is hysterical and will not be soothed.

There she stands by the battlements, trembling, weeping, a pitiful sight. Cassandra and Helen are physically very different. The Trojan woman is that thin, pale, fine-drawn type, with great black eyes, and masses of very fine black hair that in the shade can look dull and lifeless, but now, in the sun and the wind is a flood of glistening iridescent black, like oil.

'Oh Helen,' she is wailing, 'if only I had kept my bargain with Apollo, if only I had kept my head and accepted the wisdom that he was offering me, if only I learned from the Gods when it would be useful to speak out and when not – if only, if only. . .but I simply had to be a sybil, I had to be a prophetess and now look what has happened: I am doomed always to be tearing my long dishevelled hair and screaming out warnings that no one listens to – just look, what is going on now, the Wooden Horse is full of Greeks, my sixth sense tells me so, and will anyone listen? No! It is all my fault. . .if I had kept my bargain with the Gods, then perhaps there would have been no war, no black Greek ships standing there beyond the headland full of armed men who are going to kill everyone here in this palace and raze it to the ground. . . '

So she raves, tugging with both hands at her hair.

Helen leans with one elbow on the battlement and looks at her. She is smiling. Her smile is vague, because she is wondering if she has been wrong never to have her golden hair flying around in luscious gleaming clouds? She wears it up, piled in complicated, or simple, masses; and she and the maids who do it for her always think, smiling, sharing the smile, of how every man who sees her that day will be dreaming of how he would like slowly to take down that

25

golden mass, coil by coil. . . No, Helen decides, she was right always to have it properly done, her hair is heavy, thick, and would never fly about distractingly, like Cassandra's light fine stuff.

Helen is listening with half an ear to Cassandra. She half turns away from her, looking out to the black ships which are slowly approaching, and will soon be standing just off the beaches where, that night, as soon as it is dark, they will disgorge their load of armed men. She is a handsome, strong woman, full of healthy flesh, with a fascination about her that is not to be explained by the bare facts of how she looks: tall, strong, well-formed, with golden hair and brown eyes (and so on). Even now, with most of the inhabitants of the palace weeping in barricaded bedrooms – because not everyone is blind and deaf and apparently unable to connect the sounds coming from inside the Wooden Horse with the imminent killing, raping and burning – Helen is careful to keep her face covered with a veil, and does not allow her beautiful arm to slip naked from under the folds of her white gown – she knows that her beauty is enhanced by concealment, to be seen only in intoxicating glimpses. Somebody might be watching, hidden behind a buttress or something.

She finds Cassandra raving on and on a terrible trial, though she is fond of the woman. What an egotist! What self-importance! She makes a song and dance – literally! – about the slightest thing. Take those snakes: she, Helen, often slips off to one of the many shrines near Troy, to visit the Gods (her kith and kin) where the sacred serpents come to greet her, winding about her neck and her arms, licking her eyelids and her lips, hissing her news of that other world which lies unseen all about us, of course – but

26

you don't have to go on and on about it, the way Cassandra does. . .

Cassandra chants on. . .'Blood, blood, I see blood. . .'

Well, naturally, thinks Helen, wondering if Menelaus can see her up there on the windy towers.

She begins to sing, softly, smiling: it is a song she is fond of. An old song. . .Helen does not know how old, nor do the inhabitants of either Troy or Greece, who love this song, and often sing it.

There is a tale to the effect that Troy has been sacked before, and Helen supposes that this song is about that time.

Close your gates, oh men of Troy (or Greece, or Sparta, or whatever.)

The enemy's black ships are close.

Like wolves they run towards us,

Black wolves with shining teeth. . .

In fact Troy has already been built and then sacked and burned to the ground six times. (Homer's was the seventh Troy.) Helen does not know this repeated calamity has been blurred to make one, generic, calamity. The records of these lands are all verbal, the memory of man is in tales, songs, and what is passed down from one generation to another, 'Listen, children, and I will sing to you of our past, the past of our glorious city, windy Troy, the jewel of these coasts, where every man is brave and every woman a beauty. Listen – happiness was ours, and wealth, and peace, but then the armed black ships of our enemies appeared around the headland and like wolves they. . .' Sacked the city. Once. Not six times, not time after time. Embarrassing really to keep records of this happening, again and again. And again. As if our glorious ancestors

27

didn't have a grain of common sense between them, or enough to stop it all happening again. And again. You'd think that once would be enough, wouldn't you?

No, Troy was sacked once before, it is in all our tales and legends. It was sacked, oh woe, alas, and the black ships. . .

How would Helen have responded if told, 'Troy, this city where you have been a captive for ten years, has been sacked and burned six times before. How do you feel about that?' She does not at once take it in. Time is opening up behind her, the past is becoming long, dim – she cannot see its end. Until this moment, she has almost believed that the past did not go back very much further than her own life. Six times – she thinks, feeling the battlements shake under her. Six times this city has arisen from the dust of previous cities. . .*and I wasn't here*. She checks her panic, makes herself smile, and nods: Yes, life is like that. Has anything ever happened in my life that lasted, that wasn't caused and then overturned by war? – No, she is not really surprised.

Then imagine saying, 'Helen, after this, the seventh destruction of Troy, it will arise, and be besieged and burned to the ground three more times: ten Troys in all, and then there will be a pile of rubble which the wind will bury in dust.' This hits her even harder. She really does feel this strong and beautiful body of hers is immortal, even when her intelligence tells her it is not. *Three more times, and I won't be here, won't be part of it all*. . . She shudders, cold in the hot sunlight which is chilling a little as the night approaches that will see this seventh Troy in flames. But it is too difficult to keep, the sudden real knowledge of her mortality. She lets it go, sets her healthy pulses going slow and calm, and thinks: Troy's death may be close, but mine is a long way off.

A long, long life is ahead of her, she is sure of it. A new stage in it is about to start. Tonight. In a few hours.

'The black ships are standing in the searoads off Troy,' raves Cassandra, her black hair whipping about in the wind. 'Oh, the dead, the dead, that will lie heaped here on these battlements, oh, the blood that will run in rivers from every portal of my father's palace. . . oh dear, oh dear. . .'

Helen, sighing, turns her beautiful head towards her. She looks long at Cassandra, and smiles. It is a slow, secret smile, full of memory. She is thinking of the night she was snatched away from her father's palace to come here – the thrill of it, the excitement. She is thinking how, as soon as it is properly dark, she will set the lamp in her bedroom window. Soon in this palace which is silent now, stunned with terror, there will ring out the shouts of the men as they tumble out of the Wooden Horse in the great hall below, the clang of their armour, the shouts and clamour of the other Greeks racing up the shore from the black ships to the gate that will already be opening, pulled back by the hands of their secret allies. The tumult! The screams, the *screams*, making the blood race! – and then the bitter tang of smoke and the crackle of the flames. She will step coolly out of her chamber, over the corpse of her husband, smiling at Menelaus, and at Odysseus, the men who killed him. The smell of blood will be making her heart beat, and dilating her pupils. As the three turn to run down a secret stairway out of the palace to the beach and the ships, she will put her hand briefly into Odysseus's hand, and brush her lips

29

against Menelaus's mouth: he will groan, Odysseus will laugh. . .

Helen, smiling, will run her tongue softly over her lips.

That smile . . . Cassandra sees it. She really sees it, sees Helen, all of her, as she stands smiling there. Cassandra stops wailing. She gazes silently and long at this woman, Helen, her friend, her enemy. She shudders. She hides her face.

PART TWO

*The Wind Blows
Away Our Words*

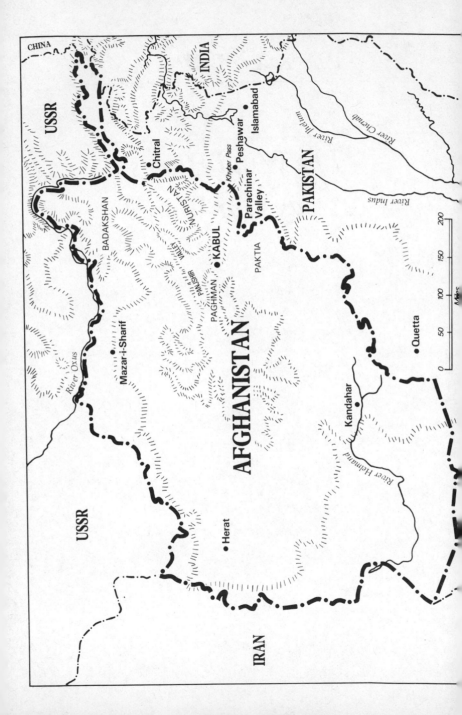

AUTHOR'S NOTE

Russia has been expanding southwards for centuries. Its ambition to conquer or influence Afghanistan long pre-dates the 1917 Revolution. 'The Great Game' – that is, who was to dominate Afghanistan – was played out through the nineteenth century between two Empires: Great Britain and Russia. The Afghans three times defeated and drove back the British. After the 1917 Revolution the Soviet Union invaded and conquered several bordering Moslem States, until it shared frontiers with Iran and Afghanistan. The Afghans see the invasion of their country as part of a long-planned and continuing expansion south. The Soviet Union was involved in intrigue in Afghanistan during the reign of Zahir Shah, at the time of the Daud takeover, and in the communist coup of 1979.

It was in 1979 that the refugees began to flow out of Afghanistan into Iran and Pakistan, and the Resistance to the communists, seen as Russian pawns, began. It was clear that the puppet government of Nur Mohammed Taraki could not survive, and the Soviet Union invaded with 100,000 troops. The Resistance – called 'the Jihad' by the Afghans, the Holy War – intensified, with all Afghanistan rising against the Russians, who responded with sophisticated and powerful weapons: MI 24 helicopters, MIG jets, tanks, heavy artillery. The most horrifying weapons are the antipersonnel bombs disguised as toys or fruit. The hospitals of Pakistan are full of children with hands and feet blown off.

The Resistance has never weakened. Although to begin with there were no weapons except for what they could capture from the Russians, the warriors of the Resistance – known as the muhjahidin – have never stopped fighting, although some western journalists have seemed anxious to claim, again and again, that the war is over, the muhjahidin defeated. The War has now gone on for seven years, three years longer than the Second World War. For most of this time the muhjahidin have fought without aid from outside, though very recently more arms have been reaching them; never enough, however, and never as much as the western powers, particularly America, have claimed. Some of the most extraordinary battles of our time have been fought between armies of modern tanks, and ragged men, women and children armed with home-made grenades, catapults, stones, ancient rifles – and the Afghans have won, again and again. The Afghans have even brought down helicopters with hand grenades tied to kites.

Beautiful parts of Afghanistan have been reduced to desert; ancient towns, full of art treasures bombed flat. One out of three Afghans is now dead or in exile or living in a refugee camp. And the world remains largely indifferent.

As one muhjahid commander, the famous Abdul Haq, Afghani, said: 'The only really hard thing is this: in the beginning we felt the whole world was with us, now we know we are alone.'

I have been associated with the Afghan struggle for some

years, through Afghan Relief, which is an unusual charity, in that no money at all is spent on administration or distribution. Every penny given gets to the refugees. I went out to visit the refugee camps in Pakistan in September 1986, together with other people associated with Afghan Relief.

*   *   *

The Air Pakistan office in Piccadilly was where the strangeness began, for that was where I sat for an hour or so to see what I could see; which was mostly orderly family groups of Pakistanis going home on holiday. Each family group created a strong private place in the public office. The women with their men seemed far from suppressed, telling them Do this, Do that. At the service points there were girls and men and the girls were every one Miss World. Unlike the brisk, comradely girls of the West these were firmly centred on femininity and tended to lapse into dark, abstracted, private thought, with sighs, pouts, bridlings implicit, even in the issuing of a ticket. And there were their veils, those coquettish wisps, always being adjusted, slipping, and sliding, needing languid readjustment.

At Heathrow the plane was late leaving by two hours, and we got to know each other, the way such crowds do. The family groups were still holding their shape, but only just: groups of men stood about; women sat in twos and threes and gossiped, calling their children who were bored and running around everywhere. There were three of us white people; two were middle-aged Scandinavians, aid workers: they had the patient look of much-tested benevolence. We eyed each other – politely of course. I, for

35

one, was thinking that white people start to look effaced, dulled, dimmed, when in a throng of these noisy, brightly dressed people. Each Pakistani woman, of whatever age, wore the slight, usually transparent veil looped around her tresses and I watched expressive painted hands arranging pretty gauzes and chiffons to show calculated amounts of hair, neck, face.

In the queue to board the plane a giggly Pakistani teenager told me she had been with her sister for a month in Scotland and they had been out every night. Where to? McDonald's, she said; and the cinema – exotic delights to her, as I was soon to discover. She did not want to go home. Defiantly bareheaded, she stared at men, who ignored her.

When the plane at last left, in no time shoes were off, veils were loose and we had become a flying caravanserai, very unlike, let's say, British Airways. What a good time I could have had, but alas, what happened was what nearly always happens when I fly. Going to Perth recently, I was seated next to a tiny crone in village black, more likely to be attending sheep, or hitting a donkey up a mountain path. She had on her chest a plaque announcing that she was so-and-so travelling to visit her nephew in Sydney, and would we all please help her. Signed: the Jordan Red Cross. Grinning and delighted she talked and talked, knowing that I couldn't understand a word. Was she saying something of importance? Various Arab speakers were summoned who said, one and all, that she spoke some dialect unknown to them. If she was announcing distress, so be it, nothing we could do; and she talked on and on. When I flagged I put my hand gently across her mouth and closed my eyes. She then remained quiet for all

36

of ten minutes, when she dug me in the ribs, laughing, and started up again. This went on for the twenty hours of the flight, past Abu Dhabi and Singapore. A kindly Canadian couple took turns with me at listening. Was she crazy? Not at all, merely determined to drink life's cup to the very lees.

On the flight to Pakistan my window seat was usurped by a forceful matron with whom I knew better than to tangle. Between her and me sat a tiny senile old man, presumably her father, who kept dropping off to sleep. Then his head slid sideways on to her shoulder, and she would push it firmly in my direction. When his head came to rest on my shoulder I pushed it back on to hers. She and I never looked at each other, we just went on doing this throughout the flight. When he was awake she conversed with him merrily. They had plenty to say. Sometimes his hand wandered over on to my lap or my food tray, and then I put it back on to his lap.

At Islamabad Airport we had to wait at Customs because a family was bringing in enough goods to furnish a large house. The wife was ordering her husband and sons around in a high commanding voice. Near me the welfare workers, who turned out to be Danes, were making knowledgeable remarks about how much this family would have to pay the official: they probably reckoned on giving him one of the TV sets, they said. This couple was off to Gilgit, a romantic place; but the weather was bad up there and they had to wait till tomorrow or the next day for a flight into the mountains.

There were five hours to fill in before the flight to Peshawar. I sat in the restaurant and watched a sample of the social life of the town, for this is where people come to enjoy themselves: there are not many ways of enjoying yourself in puritan Pakistan. In those hours there was only one mixed group: two young men, their wives and their children; otherwise it was all groups of men and groups of women sitting separately. The young men were sedate and drank very strong tea and ate cakes and conversed. (Did this brew of concentrated tannin, milk, and sugar originate in India, to be taken home to Britain by the servants of the Raj? Or was it evolved in Britain, and taken to India where it survives? – though in Britain it is on its way out, being replaced by coffee and a range of weaker, genteel teas.) Twice, groups of old men in turbans came in, filled long tables and ate large meals, hardly speaking. The women in groups had a much jollier time than the men; loudly talking and laughing. They arrived veiled, the lower parts of their faces tightly covered, then the veils fell down but were not replaced. When the women left they veiled themselves.

I was going to Peshawar up in the north-west of Pakistan because this is the centre of activites for the eastern part of Afghanistan; the centre for the western half is Quetta. I had spent months reading books and articles about Afghanistan in which Peshawar, an enticing town born to be the setting for a Bogart movie, figures large, but seldom is it mentioned that Peshawar is the centre only for the eastern side of Afghanistan. It is as if the American eastern states claimed to be all America. The journalists do not much go to Quetta (a dreary little place I'm told), but this means that activities in the western part of Afghanistan are less often mentioned. Also, to get into Afghanistan from Peshawar means going through the lands of the Pushtuns. Some journalists seem to think that the Pushtuns comprise all of Afghanistan's population. Indeed, one otherwise admirable book says so; it is as if Texas were to be seen as all of the United States.

I had been involved in Afghan Relief for some years and had been invited to come and see for myself, so as to write articles about the conditions of the refugees and about the muhjahidin, among whom, rumours said, were women fighting in all-female groups. They were supposed to have their own organization, training, sources of supply. I hoped to contact them. This never happened and the trip turned out differently. 'Going to Peshawar?' I had been told, 'Don't bother to expect anything because it won't happen.'

The landscape is brown and dusty. Not like Africa when you look down from the plane and see it brown and dusty from horizon to horizon. Not like Australia, all brown dust, and, during the hours of travelling from west to east coast, marked out in rectangles of large scale ownership. Nor is it like Texas where the brown rectangles are so large. Here it is like nothing I remember, for every inch of this landscape is cultivated in a multitude of tiny terraces, lots and plots and fields that are not rectangular or square but have rounded ends; or are curved and lapped like patterns of fish scales, or like feathers lying softly one against the other. The patterns of cultivation are a modest effort of human reclamation against savage erosion: it looks as if great claws have raked this land again and again but the people have come back and made their little fields over the gulleys and the ridges. From Islamabad to Peshawar it takes thirty minutes and you wish the little aeroplane would stand still in the air and let you gaze and take in the intricacies of this landscape reclaimed from dust. They say that when Alexander the Great's armies came down through here there were forests. They say that in the twelfth century you could walk from Malaga to Barcelona and never leave the shade of trees. When I was in Iceland this year they said that there had been trees, the little, stubborn, twisted trees of Iceland, until the invading Norsemen's goats laid bare the soil. The ancient and legendary city of Peshawar is over two thousand years old, says the guidebook, and so once it must have spread among forests and rivers. Probably this plain was first settled because of all these great rivers coming down from the Himalayas, coiling and forking between the fields. Perhaps for centuries this plain was full of villages made of mud on river banks and among trees. We are approaching Peshawar: what are those strange-looking villages down there? They are not like the villages near Islamabad: the houses seem stubby and effaced, as if a great thumb has rubbed across them – later I hear these are the Afghan refugee villages which were built by piling up the wetted earth to make walls, as children make mud houses: as people all over the world for thousands of years have made houses from earth. Their need was urgent and great, so the houses went up quickly and are fragile, vulnerable.

The aircraft goes in a wide sweep over the plain with the Himalayas on one side and the strong evening sun shining orange through a thick haze of pollution. Coming in low, you can see that often, on the roof of one of these fragile mud houses, is a tent or a hut with yet more people, more refugees from The Catastrophe, which is what the Afghans call the Russian invasion.

Peshawar struck me as all confusion, noise, traffic, a

ramshackle haphazard place; but a friend who knows India says that Pakistani cities are cleaner, richer and better-kept. There are hardly any beggars, no obvious poverty, no people living in the streets. Peshawar's population has doubled because of the refugees. When the refugees first started to pour in seven years ago there were Pakistanis who divided their houses and everything they had with them, saying this was their duty according to the laws of God. There are now probably three and a half million refugees, mostly around Peshawar.

This has happened here before; the history of the plain is of continual invasions, conquests, over-runnings. Peshawar was once part of Afghanistan, was used by its rulers as an escape from whatever inclement weather was afflicting them, cold or hot. Peshawar has also belonged to the Pushtuns, who regard themselves now as being boxed into their present territory, their rightful land taken from them. This naturally makes the Pakistanis uneasy: former conquerors are now their guests, or contained, resentful, on their borders.

All over Peshawar, amongst amiable Pakistanis, stride the muhjahidin, hundreds of thousands of them. Westerners think they all look like bandits and are titillated or put off. They wear the baggy pants which one of us, donning them, says is the coolest garb ever invented, with currents of air flowing around you as you move. Then the long loose shirt to knee level, and a blanket slung over one shoulder which is their bedding, their covering, their tent. They sometimes wear waistcoats. I saw one in good quality English tweed with the selvedge 'Made in Britain' used as decoration. Sometimes the waistcoats are embroidered. They wear the little Afghan pillbox hats by themselves, or with a turban around them, or the Afghan berets. The

41

turbans are many and amazing. If these men are not carrying Kalashnikovs, and they are not supposed to carry them in cities, it is as if they are shouldering imaginary weapons. These fierce men may seem to have come out of another century, and in some ways they have, but they are well informed about what is going on in the world. They have no idea how to present themselves sympathetically to the westerner, going into all kinds of heroic postures, talking about martyrdom, dying for their faith, Paradise with maidens and pretty boys and wine, and so on and so forth. When photographed they adopt warrior-like postures. They do this because they think this is what will impress. Talking ordinarily they do not use this kind of bravado. They are a sensible, non-fanatical people; or at least the ones I met were. I did not meet any of the extreme and bigoted mullahs, and their followers, but judging from some television programmes and some articles, there are those who have met no other kind of Afghan. They have that brand of sardonic humour special to people up against it: black and wry and shocking – like Jewish humour. These warriors move in and out of Peshawar from the battles that take place all the time over the eastern part of Afghanistan. They rest and they feed themselves up, they give wounds time to heal, they visit their families in the refugee camps. They bring letters and messages. You will see two or three, or a group, of muhjahidin meeting in a street: hugs and kisses all round, they are relieved to see each other alive – these comrades who they last saw or heard of in battle. Their comradeship is strong; war comradeship, quite apart from the comradeship of Islam, which is another subject. This closeness is attractive to watch from outside and I'd take a bet that when the war is over these men will all be talking about the best years of their lives. When they are thinking of how they are presenting themselves to you, the word 'Jihad' is used in every sentence. This is their word for their Resistance and it does not mean simply the 'Holy War'. It is like 'The Resistance' in France in the last war. They all intend to fight the Russians back out of their country; they say things like, 'We fought the Arabs for a hundred years before they finally defeated us, and we'll fight the Russians for as long.' The muhjahidin have a hard life and often a short one. If badly wounded in battle they do not survive: there are all those great mountains to cross to reach hospitals. The boys growing up in the camps are their replacements. Every boy you see longs to be off with his father, his brothers, but some commanders won't let them fight until they are sixteen. Mahsud, for example, continually besieged by boys begging to fight, sends them back to their families. (Mahsud is a commander admired all over Afghanistan by nearly all the muhjahidin, even when they are members of different parties. He is the nearest thing to a national leader to have evolved in this war.)

The Afghans do not resemble the Pakistanis in anything: they are a hard mountain people built for survival; warriors and proud of being able to live off less than what softer people need. Before The Catastrophe all visitors to Afghanistan fell in love with the Afghans, as if with their own fabled past, when we were proud, tough, brave, independent, and witty and generous as well. Why are the Afghans so very good-looking, all of them? A reply can be the grim one: that so many of them die in their first year, we are seeing the survival of the fittest and handsomest.

The Pakistanis are also beautiful people in a different way: easy, charming, good-natured. . .and lazy. Sitting in an office full of Pakistani men (no women of course), you realize offices can exist to provide men with jobs. We sat in a large shabby room with dirty windows, while the fan revolved slowly overhead – I'd swear these fans are hypnotic and slow the mind. The room is crammed with ancient desks. Two manual typewriters. (Why not? I use one myself.) About ten men sit around doing nothing at all, drinking tea, gossiping. They regard with tentative friendliness these disconcerting western guests, who include three women wearing their immodest clothes. (From our point of view, we were trying hard, keeping arms and necks covered, wearing trousers or long skirts.) We were requesting permits, one for the Parachinar Valley which is almost surrounded by Afghanistan. The chief official does not want to give us one. He says a battle is going on there. But a muhjahid commander has just told us there was a battle, but it is over. When we tell him this, the official says that if we are all kidnapped by the Russians, Pakistan will be held responsible. But we know that journalists are always going in and out of Afghanistan. We have been told by a journalist that the road after dusk is a highway full of muhjahidin, villagers, spies of all kinds, traders bringing goods to the bazaars of Peshawar, and, of course, journalists. There is a Peshawar joke that an enterprising American is setting up a travel agency for trips with the muhjahidin into Afghanistan. The bureaucratic tussle goes on, and is eventually settled in another more important office. Meanwhile we talk to these men. They want to know where we come from: they would all like to visit London, Texas, Stockholm. One asks if

London is in England. We joke about cowboys and oil wells. They are likable, these people, and I could look at them forever, men and women, so handsome and good humoured and sleek are they. Not that one gets much chance to see the women. Leaving, my strongest memory was of groups of men standing around, sitting around, lounging in streets, on pavements, against cars, and staring at women, at the three of us. One elderly – me; one a blonde from Texas, continually besieged by Pakistanis, so beguiling do they find fair hair and blue eyes; and a beautiful girl of Afghan origin but brought up in England. That long, hard, dark stare: we all tried to analyse it. What can it mean? Hostility? Curiosity? Dislike? It is as if these men switch off as human beings for the time they look at you. It is frightening. Sometimes they jeer or laugh, but more often it is the prolonged, dark, distant stare at the alien. But these same men become friendly and helpful as soon as you appeal to them – become a person.

Unless you have influence, and everything works on influence, on whom you know, impressions of Peshawar and of the Afghan Resistance are determined often by luck; what groups of muhjahidin do you meet? Which political Party will befriend you? There are seven political parties among the exiled Afghans, all based on Islam and the Koran, ranging from the bigotry of the Fundamentalists to the liberal modern attitudes of Hiriquat.

Journalists swarm, a fascinating study in themselves. Many are drawn by temperament to the place, a romantic, seedy little town swarming with arms and drugs dealers and spies, adventurers of all kinds. There are hotels and bars where journalists congregate. KHAD agents, who have placed themselves just behind you, their backs to you, tilt their chairs towards you, as in a comic opera, if some subject of interest is introduced; and it is said the mischievous start whole tangles of false information just for the hell of it. (KHAD is the Secret Service of the puppet Afghan government, trained and maintained by the Russians.)

The spies of Peshawar are famed for being able to accommodate multiple allegiances, two, three, or more, at the same time. KHAD, the Russians themselves, foreign governments, the competing Afghan political parties in exile, all spy on each other, on the muhjahidin, on the refugees, and on visiting journalists and aid workers.

There are huge numbers of young journalists sent there to cut their teeth. Unkindly I'd say: a painful apprenticeship. Any Moslem country is difficult for a westerner. We were fighting them for a thousand years. We are full of ignorance and prejudice and so are they. It is unfortunate that the West, particularly America, associates the words 'Islam', Moslem' with 'Terrorist', or with Fundamentalist Islam, such as we read about in connection with Khomeini and Ghadafi. This is only one strand of Islam and not, in my view, the most important one, though it may, alas, become the most important. Pakistan is not Fundamentalist like, let's say, Iran – not anywhere near.

Islamic countries are very different from each other and laws that sound the same are different in practice. Let's take a sentence of fifty lashes. In Iran or Saudi Arabia this will be as savage as it sounds. In Pakistan the extremes of Islam are softened (and will modify further if the bigots are kept out of power). The punisher must use a padded whip, and hold a Koran between his side and his upper arm: the Koran must not fall out as he wields the whip. Some laws seem to us absurd. Pakistan is 'dry'. Predictably, this means there is clandestine drinking: people not used to drinking don't drink well, and often this is not a pretty sight. If you are a foreigner you may drink, but there is no fun in it if you have to sign permits and drink hidden in your hotel room. One of the reasons westerners may drink is that it is known wine is part of our religious practice: a friend of mine emerging from a bar in a hotel was asked by a perhaps wistful waiter if the religious ceremony had been satisfactory. Attitudes to women are not consistent, but, I am told, hardening. A conventional woman is probably content, she is secure enough. I've heard them hectoring and bullying their men in ways I found repellent – the slave's revenge? But a talented, ambitious, or independent woman: for her it must be hell. Just as it was in Victorian England. A woman journalist, unless she knows the languages, faces every kind of difficulty because of the attitudes of the men. A man journalist cannot meet the women in the refugee camps. The camps and the muhjahidin are what the journalists come for. The muhjahidin all belong, nominally at least, to one of the seven parties. These are not remotely like anything we have in the West, and are hard for a westerner to understand, being based on religion; and they bicker, intrigue, and compete over issues we think petty, even silly.

The muhjahidin will willingly take journalists in; not far it is true, but this is because of the nature of their visitors who, on the whole, they tend to despise because of our softness. If heroism has been your chief weapon for seven years then heroism is what you value most. They tell scornful stories of film makers demanding to photograph battles and who, when a battle starts, dive for cover. A muhjahid will then take the camera himself and film the action. Or of doctors who cannot keep up with them, who cannot exist on the minimal levels of food the muhjahidin need, who have to have special food and shelter, and have been known to faint at the sight of the terrible injuries caused in these battles. For this reason, the softness of the doctors, the muhjahidin prefer friendly countries to provide teams of doctors who will train selected muh-jahidin in basic medical skills, so they may attach them-selves to groups of fighters going in to Afghanistan. They complain that journalists will refuse offers of journeys to Kabul, Mazar-i-Sharif, and the Liberated Areas, pre-ferring to go in close to the border, let's say, Kandahar, or with the Pushtuns. As a commander said, 'if you go to Bahrain for a holiday, why not Kabul? We control it.' Yes, they're a flamboyant lot, but they break your heart, they are so brave and have so little: even now most of their weapons are captured from the Russians.

'Have you been *in*?' you hear one breathless neophyte ask another in Green's Hotel or in Dean's Hotel. Both these hotels you'd think were built as sets for cloak-and-dagger films. I would say that going *in* to Pushtun land (the Pathans), usually for four or five days, is not necessarily the best way to get adequate and unbiased information: you will hear only the opinions of the group that takes you. You won't get in at all if no group likes you enough. A certain frustrated young woman journalist recently exclaimed that she was going to Delhi, the only place to get real information! The day after we, in our group, heard a high-up person in one of the parties explain that he would like to assist any journalist with serious intentions, there was an article in the *Pakistan Times* saying that the muhjahidin were tired of taking in so many journalists at so much risk to themselves and with so little return for it all. Not easy, any of it, and certain levels of information are out of reach to most.

With our group was an Afghan from Paghman, with relatives and friends fighting with muhjahidin or working in Afghan Relief. Then an Afghan girl brought up in England: she is learning journalism in Peshawar and speaks Farsi, Arabic, some Urdu. A Swedish film maker, Leon Flamholc: his forebears came from Uzbekistan and in muhjahid dress he becomes a muhjahid. He speaks Farsi. He was 'in' on a previous trip to Peshawar and he had a film half finished. A woman film maker from Texas, Nancy Shiels, was on her third trip, with a half-finished film. And there was myself. I have been involved with Afghans for some years but had not been in Pakistan. (I was born in Persia and lived there until I was five. Yes, all kinds of scents and sounds came back.)

From the moment you arrive in Peshawar, Afghanistan enfolds you – the enormity of it, the horror, the sadness. From early morning to late at night it is what you talk about, think about – in my case what you dream about. Every Afghan you meet, muhjahid or refugee, is another tragic story: each one is an appeal: Help us, help us! We in the West are ill-informed they say, otherwise we would be helping them. This illustrates one of the little ironies that makes it tempting to believe in Gods who still sit somewhere up there laughing at us. From the start of this war the Russians have claimed, and might even believe, that the West, mainly America, has financed the Resistance in Afghanistan. Russian soldiers are told that they are going to fight against American Imperialists, (even American

Zionist Imperialists – a nice twist), the Chinese; the bandits of international capital. They find ragged and bare-footed men with Kalashnikovs, stolen from them. Some defect because of this, but 'Don't exaggerate this,' says a muhjahid commander, 'one per cent perhaps are upset enough to defect to us, the rest are Soviet-minded and they are taught to see us as animals to be hunted down and killed.' Seven years after the war started, the muhjahidin still appropriate most of their weapons from the Russians. The muhjahidin say that when the US first denied that they were sending aid they did it in such a way as to sound as if they were in fact supplying aid but had to deny it. Now the muhjahidin say yes, aid is being sent, but what happens to it? They get very little of what is being sent. It is the major theme of every conversation with every muhjahid commander. I expected this, having read of it. 'We are fighting for you as well as for ourselves,' they say. 'The Russians want what they've always wanted: to gain access to the warm water ports and to take what is now Pakistan. Why do you not aid us? It is in your interests to do so.'

The theme that beats through every conversation, every interview, is this one: 'From the very beginning the West has under-estimated the extent of the Resistance. We have been reading for seven years, and often from your leading journalists, that we are finished, ready to give up. This has never been true. You describe us as if we are passive under the Russians, occasionally making little hit-and-run raids – not as we are: a nation continuously at war; with everyone involved. Would you like to see for yourselves?'

We sat all morning in the headquarters of a certain political party while the muhjahidin commanders came in from all over eastern Afghanistan from north to south, three at a time, to sit for a while, answer questions and then to make way for others. They came from Paghman and the Parachinar; from Baghlam and Bagram, from Kabul and Paktia; there were Turkomans from Mazar-i-Sharif and from Badakstan with their Chinese war lord faces; and from Nuristan, who sometimes look astonishingly as if they have just come from Scotland or from Kent. The Nuristanis claim to be descendants of Alexander the Great's armies but these armies swept over all Afghanistan, as did the Mongols and the Arabs. The British, the last invaders, did not get very far; we were three times beaten by those warriors. (History: three men are talking: 'My ancestors were Mongols, yours Arabs, the Afghans fought us and now we all together, like brothers, fight the Russians to the death.') One commander just in from fighting near Mazar-i-Sharif has come to get new ammunition: 'It was a big battle; jets, helicopters. They come in from over the borders and run away back there. They fight like cowards, they bomb us from a great height. They have burned all the crops, they waited until they were ripe because they wanted to destroy our supply basis with the people. It takes a month to get a consignment of arms and food from Peshawar to the Oxus, everywhere we have to watch out for the Russian 'toys' – bombs disguised as watches or pens or like small children's toys. They are dropped in the paths where they know we may walk.' The hospitals in the camps are full of children without arms, hands, feet, legs because of these toys they can't resist. Another commandant from the extreme north tells how he and his band cut the pipelines carrying kerosene, gas, petrol: 'We destroy them again and again, the Russians

51

can't keep them in repair, they can only guard them in the middle of the day for we control the night.' We say, 'We are reporters from America and from England, is there a message you would like to give to the West?'

'Where are the arms? We have even been fighting with axes.' (We thought this might be an exaggeration. The muhjahidin are accused of poetic exaggeration – people say that what they tell has to be taken with a grain of salt, but later on this detail was confirmed by someone else fighting in this particular battle.) 'We have no food, we have been chewing wool and leather. We do this until we grow weak and have to end a battle, even when we're winning.'

Another commander from the north says that they have their families and dependents in caves in the hills with horses and donkeys. Their villages have been razed, there's nothing left of them, the irrigation systems destroyed. To each fighter there are five dependents, they take it in turns to go to the front in units of a hundred: 'We have no medicines, no doctor, no food. Yes, we capture some from the Russians, but often the Russian medicines are things we have never seen: hypodermics and drugs, we don't know how to use them.'

A commander from Kabul says, 'We have two organizations, one for inside Kabul and one out. The one inside is a sabotage organization; everyone in Kabul is on our side and that is why the Russians can't catch us. The women help us, even the children. We have people in KHAD, so many that the Russians could never catch them; and they tell us when to expect attacks and that is why we win. The Russians cannot move more than five miles from Kabul.'

And through the long morning again and again and

again, from all the commanders; it is hunger that is destroying the muhjahidin: 'We have no food, we have no warm clothes, no boots, only sandals. We lose our feet and hands from frostbite. In some places people are already starving and it is only autumn, there is the whole of the winter to come. Send us food, send us warm clothes. If you supplied us with ground-to-air missiles we would defeat the Russians, why do you not do this?'

And, continually repeated: 'The West say we are disunited because you are seeing things through your eyes. You are always looking for a single command over all Afghanistan, that is why you are always building up Mahsud or Hakkani, or another, speculating whether he will become a national leader; it is not the Afghan way. We have area leaders, they respect each other and work together but it is not likely that there will evolve a national leader.'

All these points were confirmed in an interview with a high-up military man in one of the parties. He would not be photographed or filmed or recorded. He said he was only one of the many who have worked in the Afghan army under cover and who have left, when it got too dangerous, for Peshawar, to help in co-ordinating the muhjahidin battles. To our relief, for by then we were suffering from an overdose of Moslem piety, he began: 'I am a military man, not a religious one. This is the operational military headquarters of this party and I am one of the people who operate it. The men on that bench, sitting along that wall, may not look to your eyes like high-ranking commanders because none of us wears uniforms.' A dozen men in the muhjahid garb sat watching. 'They are not members of this particular party, and you may care to draw your

53

conclusions from that, I will answer all your questions and I will tell you nothing but the truth, but journalists do a very great deal of damage because few realize how much use an enemy can make of some apparently unimportant detail. You have not been trained in Intelligence, I have. It is not your fault, but I shall be protecting our positions as we talk.'

'The main point, the key point, is that the war is going on at full strength whatever you may have heard. It is not going badly, as your newspaper sometimes claim. We will not stop fighting, we will fight until we win and the Russians leave, or until they kill us all. This is the basic and important fact. None of you in the West seem to have any idea of the extent of the Resistance; every house, every village is involved. If an area is quiet for a time, that does not mean it is subdued, only waiting, perhaps because of the weather.'

We asked about co-ordination between the different areas of Afghanistan, the different parties:

'Two aspects, the military first: there are parts of Afghanistan where a commander may have under him men from all the political parties and it has been like that since the beginning of the war. In other parts groups of muhjahidin may fight each other, and there is every degree between these two extremes, But even the most stubborn and fanatical muhjahidin have come to understand that they must co-operate to win. There are generally respected leaders, of whom of course you have heard, and they co-operate with each other. The political aspect is as important; pressure is coming on the seven political parties from two directions: from the outside as, for example, when aid is given on condition the parties co-operate on a certain issue; and, perhaps more importantly, from inside. The muhjahidin are weary of ideological bickering between the factions. There is a third aspect which I am sure there is no need to elaborate, for it is a problem everywhere and in every country: it is the problem of personality clashes, which in our case is exacerbated by the very great difference in ideological outlook. Nothing is easy in this struggle and this question of ideology is perhaps the most difficult. The people you in the West call Fundamentalists are the most ideological but they are also the best of the fighters, they began fighting before any other group did. They have allies and followers all over the Moslem world and, long-term, this may create difficulties for us all. I feel sure that you will have heard this subject discussed during your stay here, for it is much on all our minds. The other main group of fighters is as large but less unified. They would like a return to the Afganistan before The Catastrophe, where differences of Islamic inter-pretation may exist side by side. This kind of tolerance is foreign to the Fundamentalists. A point of interest is that more clashes take place inside the Fundamentalist groups than in any of the others. The problems arising from the clashes between personalities exist in every kind of group.'

'Would you care to give us a strategic bird's eye view of this war?'

'I will of course not give you a full answer to that question and you cannot expect it. For one thing it would be too complicated to do so. I have been in this struggle from the first day in different ways. I could write not one book, but several on this very involved and intricate history. I can tell you today that there are three major areas of fighting: Herat, Kabul, and Kandahar, but this will not be true by this time next week; there will be new areas of fighting. Enemy pressure has increased in the last year fivefold, there are more troops, more sophisticated weapons, the Russians are using better tactics and much greater ruthlessness. The casualties and destruction of material is greater on their side than ever and on our side is much suffering and many casualties. You have been told that 80% of Afghanistan is controlled by the muhjahidin, 20% by the Russians. From one point of view that is true, but from a military point of view it is more useful to think like this: 100% of Afghanistan is controlled by the Russians and 100% by us – who is going to strike next and where? The Russians cannot do as they like, even in the cities which they claim to control, they never know where or what will be blown up. They cannot move freely along the main roads; the main roads are dangerous for them and we cannot use them either, but then we can operate on every kind of terrain and they cannot. We control the Liberated Areas but the Russians will send their bombers in to destroy a place if something doesn't suit them. They destroy our crops there and our animals. They are intensifying this policy of destroying our food. As we sit here, refugees are streaming out from newly bombed areas because irrigation systems have been deliberately destroyed and the crops burned. Now you know what I mean by our both controlling Afghanistan. There are more security posts being built now than in the last three or four years, but most of them have already been encirled, destroyed, rendered useless. Morale? Their morale is low because the war goes on with no result and our morale is lower too. We have been fighting for seven years and we are tired and we feel that you do not help us. You will of

56

course have heard the muhjahidin claim that they are fighting for you; this is something that we believe, one of the reasons that we fight. It is extremely hard for us to replenish our supplies, it is hard to equip our men and to feed them. Last winter we did not stop fighting but went on and at a very great cost. Our men fight in sandals in deep snow, they fight in the clothes that they wear in the summer, they fight on little food until it runs out. In this country, in Pakistan, they will no longer accept more refugees. Our debt to Pakistan is very great, they are sorry for us, they help us as far as they can, we are grateful. But now, when the refugee trains come in after a new bombing on their villages, they may die from lack of food and water. We sometimes have more arms than we can use because of our inability to transport them.' (We had just heard a commander describe how he had captured Russian tanks and guns near Kabul but had had to destroy them all; for he had nowhere to put them.) 'We have enough of certain kinds of arms but not enough of others. As you have already been told by every muhjahid you have met, we need ground-to-air missiles, we need more money to buy what *we* know we need, not what other people think we need. We need food, we need medical supplies, we need these things fast, with winter coming. Have you been told that, whereas once the muhjahidin were given food by the peasants, now they will often give the peasants some of their own very scanty food because the people are starving?'

'The Americans – we are grateful for what they have given and are giving. We keep reading about these vast sums of money voted for us, but what happens to this money and the supplies? The Americans have expressed their support in our struggle and we must believe that they mean it, but would it not be in their interests, as well as ours, to find out where these supplies of money and arms go to? They send it, we do not receive it. In the middle there is some kind of hole into which most of these things vanish. Again and again we read in your newspapers that such and such arms have been sent – but if they have, we never see them. Generally speaking the Americans do not seem to have understood that war must be a combination of the military and the political; we are doing our part and we are doing it well, but we feel that we are not being supported adequately.'

We asked, 'Could the Russians leave?'

'You know of course that the Russians have never left any country of their own free will. If I were Gorbachev, I would not know how to leave easily after such bloodshed and such propaganda, but if some formula were found they would leave. They want to leave. No matter what they say, they know that we shall never stop fighting. I have worked with the Russians for years, I know them well. As a soldier, I admire them for their resistance in the Second World War; they are not good fighters but they were good defenders of their homes. They have no soldierly qualities, they are bad shots, they are too heavy physically, they drink too much, they cannot climb or use mountains, they have very little endurance, they are lost without their equipment, their cars, their aeroplanes. We can do without these things. They cannot match us Russian for Afghan but they send in three or four against one, they bomb us from so high we cannot reach them.

'When they use Afghan against Afghan they do not do so well. They do not understand us, they do not understand our kind of independence – if you like, anarchy – which is our strength. The kind of pressures they put on the Afghan army make it impossible for that army to use Afghan fighting qualities; they will not allow the Afghan army any initiative at all. We believe too that the Afghan army are bad fighters because their consciences are troubling them. There always comes a point when some great scheme or plan simply collapses, fails, crumbles.' (At this point a little argument developed between a man on one of the benches and another about how many in the Afghan army are happy in their work. 'Forty thousand at the very most in all the country', says one. The other says, 'Five thousand at the most. If there were more they would do better, they are useless.') 'The Russians have a certain characteristic which is to their disadvantage; if something goes badly then they do not change tactics or try something else, they simply bear down more heavily and intensify what they are already doing. They often destroy what they try to do, they are rigid and inflexible, they cannot listen, they are stubborn, and they go their own way. But then, if the Russians were subtle they would have found a way out of this war without loss of face long ago. And they choose weak people as leaders. This is a disadvantage to them in the long run. I know Najib well, he is a nothing, a weak man, how can he lead a country? He is not intelligent, no Afghan could possibly respect him. In order to understand Afghanistan you have to remember that the Afghans are the most independent people on earth. When I say that each one is a natural commander and can never be a good follower, as one who is trying to orchestrate them I say it with a certain irony.

'You will have heard, I am sure, more than you need of

Jihad, but in my view Jihad is too simple a concept, used as the West tends to use it. The Afghan fights first of all for himself, his family, his village, his own people. He fights for a combination of these reasons, and he fights for his religion. When you hear the word "Jihad", and you will have heard it a thousand times a day, remember how complex it is, this Holy War.'

We asked if it would be difficult for the muhjahidin to stop fighting and accept peace. 'Yes, very difficult; they are natural warriors. When this war ends there will be a period when personal and tribal accounts will be settled. The war will cease gradually, but there is an Afghan characteristic which you must remember: It is that when we do decide to give allegiance to a government we also give obedience. A future government must tolerate very great differences of opinion – religious and political, but there will be one difference between before the war and now: before the Russian invasion there might have been a few hundred communists; when they leave there will be none.'

We asked about attitudes towards publicity. 'Every week or ten days I make a strategic report based on information that comes in from all over Afghanistan, for we have people in every part of the country, and this is accurate information. I send this report out; we never see a word of it in your press. Some of us feel that we put a great deal of effort into allowing journalists into Afghanistan and giving out information, with very little return. My personal belief is that we need much more publicity and to make more efforts to get good films made and good journalistic reports. We, above all, need more journalists to go into Afghanistan, but not just near Peshawar, which is where they nearly all go; they need to go all over the country, and we will take them.'

'What do you think of the French journalist who described a certain muhjahidin stronghold so well that the Russians came in and bombed it as soon as his report was published?'

'That was certainly unfortunate, he was careless, as journalists often are, but in the long run it was worth it. If you people were better informed we would all be better off.'

The points made by this commander, were all corroborated in other interviews. For instance:

Q: 'You say that there are very many more Russian soldiers in Afghanistan, not less, but this goes against recent Russian claims?'

A: 'Have you never heard of the famous Russian Disinformation?'

Another commander: 'I have just read that a bomb went off in South Africa and killed nine people. I have come from a battle where we shot down a helicopter, disabled six tanks and killed thirty Russians with the loss of five muhjahidin, but that will never be in your newspapers. Would it be better perhaps if I had a black face?'

Conversation with a muhjahid just about to go back into Kabul: he says, 'Do you know perhaps of a pill we can take to still hunger; it is our worst enemy?'

A housewife's approach to the war – (mine): 'Why don't you set up a factory and make concentrated foodstuffs for the muhjahidin to carry into battle?'

'We are fighters, that is what we know.'

'Napoleon said that an army marches on its stomach.'

'If we marched on our stomachs the war would have ended by now. I myself and my men have just finished

61

fighting. For twenty days we have been fighting, our food ran out and we were filling our stomachs with grass.'

'Yes, yes, yes, yes, we know that, but if you set up a little factory, no, perhaps a series of little workshops here in Peshawar, or somewhere in your caves in the mountains and make concentrated foodstuffs, easily portable— '

'Who?'

'Well, the parties perhaps.'

'The parties! Which party? You don't know them.'

'Why not all of them together?'

'Together! They quarrel all the time! Did you know that Mahsud has just sent out an appeal to his HQ, asking for food before the winter? They didn't send him any.'

'You say that the muhjahidin are working together more and more, ignoring the parties. Why don't you, the muh-jahidin, set up little factories or workshops and make— '

'What is this stuff you are talking about?'

'In the past your own armies marched with dried com-pressed mulberries, full of calories, not for twenty days at a time of course, perhaps for three or four. What you need is to get sugar, fat, dried fruit, flour – a lot of calories, and vitamins – then when all of this is mixed together, it is compressed, so that the goodness is there but it is very small and light.'

'Very well, you send us the money, tell us how to do it, we'll do it.'

'You'll need places in several different areas, because the Russians will blow them up if they can.'

'And if they could be mobile, so much better, yes? Could we make concentrated foodstuffs for horses per-haps? Our horses and donkeys carry in our equipment and food but there is no food for them quite often and they die.'

A major theme of every conversation with the muhjahidin is that the political parties, who claim to represent he fighters, no longer do so. Aid from abroad is sent through these parties and, in order to get what little ammunition or food they do, the muhjahidin have to play along with them.

'We do the fighting, we call the tune with the Russians. The parties sit in Peshawar fighting among themselves, giving themselves fat jobs, cars, they have become bureaucracies. If we won our war tomorrow the parties would simply disappear, no one wants them.'

We had been granted an interview by the Amir Mohamedi, leader of the Hiriquat Party. Hiriquat stands for association with the West, liberal Islam, the restoration of pre-Catastrophe Afghanistan, where different interpretations of Islam flourished. (And where the mullahs were not as powerful as they have since become; extreme faiths do well in hard times, political and religious, as we have all seen.) The Amir is a mullah. I was nervous because my associations with the word 'mullah' were over-simple. I had been listening to women complain: 'The mullahs have us helpless in the refugee camps. They control what we do, and the Pakistanis allow this.' (One of the reasons why the mullahs have become so powerful is precisely this one. Pakistan has problems in policing the camps because men are not allowed into the women's quarters, while mullahs, being so saintly, are. The Pakistanis therefore use the mullahs to control the women.)

I had not – still have not – met any of these bigoted and ignorant (mostly old) men, but some of our group had filmed and interviewed them, and returned dismayed. I had been shocked by Naipaul's *Among The Believers*, but had reflected that, living in the West, I knew several Moslems, (whose religion I do not like better than any other), who are intelligent, open-minded, liberal, and who say that Islam is full of people such as they, even in countries like Iran, where they are biding their time. In Pakistan I had met others. Why – I had been wondering – had Naipaul, of the right religious background and experience to meet anyone he liked, only met religious maniacs, and in so many Moslem countries? Why do so many westerners return from forays into Islam reporting only fanaticism and intolerance? Is it that the West enjoys frightening itself with the extremes of Islam, news of the wicked Saracen, even now?

The Amir's home is a villa like any other, but its garden is far from ordinary, full of jasmine, roses, plants in pots, shady bowers: everything that an oriental garden is supposed to be. Against a background of shrubs was a low bed with a thin pallet on it, covered with a bright salmon and purple cloth, like a little throne. In front of it stretched a length of matting. We left our shoes at its edge. On the bed sat the Amir Mohamadi, crosslegged. He wore dazzling white robes and on his head a lilac checked turban like a tablecloth, tied around an elegant black and silver cap. He dangled prayer beads: his hands, I thought, were those of a man of action, of affairs: muscular, strong.

It is said that we live in 'a culture of appearances' – that more and more we all judge people by how they look. (More and more, I think, people behave to conform with how they look.) This was brought home to me by my reactions to the Mullah. I had not found it so difficult to accept that men who looked like eighteenth-century Balkan bandits talked with sophistication about world affairs, but although I had been told that he is far from the conventional western idea of a mullah, I had to struggle with a strong sense of improbability. I have read enough about Islam to know some of its basic ideas, history, and great historical figures, and was not surprised that he looked like pictures of Rumi or El-Ghazali, the very image of a medieval saint. But that he should be a modern man as well? I supposed in my crass western way that the way he looked was a PR job designed to impress the less sophisticated faithful, until, coming out of Pakistan, I asked some Moslem friends, who said, 'Oh no, my father is like that.' 'Not at all, my uncle is just like that.' And I suppose we should not be surprised when some Christian sects choose to conduct their rites in garb that makes them look like Renaissance princes, and there are Christian orders which still wear the clothes of medieval peasants.

The Amir's introductory discourse on the history of the Afghan war was concluded by, 'It is a matter of record that I started the Resistance. I came out with two friends through Quetta. We had no money, nothing. We went to the students and said will you fight? We trained commando groups, attacked eight fortified police posts. The news spread like a storm across Afghanistan and this is how the Resistance started.'

This was a long interview. These are the answers I was particularly struck by: 'If there had been no Russian invasion, what do you think Afghanistan would be like now?'

'We would be free, is this not the main thing? I am surprised you should ask. Afghanistan is not free. There are no human rights under the Russians. Progress in this field in one country belongs to the whole world. When the Rule of Law has been abolished in a country, it is a loss to the whole world. Afghanistan has regressed in all respects. We were going forward in law, human freedom, the press, communications, education. The country was already being modernized, many of our young people were being educated abroad, we had the beginnings of a technologically trained elite; things were changing very fast.'

The Amir then spoke at length about Islam, how Afghanistan could have provided a model for a liberal Islamic State. 'Islam is bound up with Afghan nationalism and this has been intensified by the war. We are not going to take anybody else's Islam when we are free again. You must remember that our Sunnis and our Shias work together; they are not split as in other Islamic countries. Before The Castastrophe Afghanistan was in no way a fanatical country; there were fanatical groups but they did not have power and were not generally respected.'

We asked: 'The Russians claim to have freed women in Afghanistan.'

He replied: 'The women were becoming free before The Catastrophe, they could choose to be veiled if they wanted and some did; or to wear jeans and sweaters if they wished. Most country women were not veiled. In the north the Tajiks, the Mongols, the Uzbeks and so on were not veiled, it is not their tradition. Is it not for Islam itself to change the status of women? Are you saying that if one country disapproves of another's policies that gives it the right to invade? Looked at historically, Islam has improved the situation of women: you have to look at certain laws in historical context. You seem to forget that you in the West have only recently, in the last half century, emerged from a bad situation as far as women are concerned. Islam is a good basis to build on. Because there are, and have been abuses, that is no reason to attack us. *It is one thing to say that Islam oppresses women, another to say that men oppress women* (my italics). The Russians oppress everyone, they offer no hope of change. We do offer hope and the basis for change. The Communists oppress minorities and religions everywhere, and no one protests. Are women the only oppressed people? Islam will reform itself and the world can help us. The way to liberate women in Afghanistan is surely not to destroy their homes and children?'

'What do you think of the present situation of the war?'

'The war is going very well, though you are being told the opposite. But we must have enough ground-to-air rockets; we are fighting for you as well. We obtain arms from anywhere we can get them, but we cannot obtain from the Russians the rockets we need to bring down the Russians. We capture almost every other kind of arms from them but we cannot get rockets.'

'The Russians take your children to the Soviet Union to be indoctrinated. Does this indoctrination go deep?'

'They are being trained to work for the Russians in Afghanistan and are being given information which they will see for themselves is false when they come home. Sovietized Afghans will be a small minority and there will be great pressure on them to change, if they do not become good Afghans. If they cannot change, then their parents will kill them. Afghans think long-term: they will not say "This is my child," but, "This is an evil person." It will be hard for the parents but they will do it.'

'The Russians say they are modernizing your country.'

'Mussolini made the trains run on time, Hitler had full employment, but nobody now admires either leader.'

'Do you get anything at all in return for the loss of your freedom?'

'Genocide.'

'What proportion of your people are Communists?'

'If there were seventy-five thousand Communists in Afghanistan when the Russians invaded, which we dispute, we have killed fifty thousand of them. If there are five thousand left then we are killing them off fast.'

We all afterwards discussed the Amir at length. An Afghan said: 'The Amir comes from an ancient family, full of poets and literary people, but with a strong military tradition. This is not an unusual combination in Afghanistan.'

We wanted to know why he became a mullah in the first place.

'You must understand that being a mullah does not mean being religious, or having a "vocation", in the western sense. A mullah is a teacher of the Law, of the traditions. It was natural for a man from such a family to become a mullah. The Amir was in Parliament for a long time, elected by his constituency. Then he became a senator. The senators were not elected, they were appointed; an advisory body, like a council of wise men.'

I heard another Afghan say sardonically, 'The Amir Mohamadi had to become a member of parliament to get heard: in the old Afghanistan it was not enough to be a mullah.'

The seven parties in Peshawar are structured, and behave like, governments in exile. Aid and arms are channelled through them, and this has given them more power than they should have. The one thing every muhjahid we met agreed on was that the fighting men all over Afghanistan have had enough of the parties. For instance: we were in a certain party HQ and a muhjahid came up to ask if anyone spoke German. He was working in Germany while his father and brothers fought in Jihad. His father was killed, his brothers asked him to go home, and he had been fighting as a muhjahid for some months. The HQ is a pleasant building, rather feminine in style, white with airy blue fretwork decorations and a pretty garden. Charming: just the place for a garden party, for lazy summer conversations; but it is swarming with warriors, muhjahidin from all over Afghanistan, We watched a white car drive up and discharge a mullah, 'There you are,' says our friend, 'that's where our money goes: cars and perks for the mullahs, jobs for pals. We fighters come in to get ammunition and have to wait while the mullahs go straight in for interviews. After waiting all day I get enough ammunition for two weeks' fighting and then I have to stop fighting and cool my heels for weeks.' And, as we hear again and again and again, 'Why don't you support us? Why don't you give us the arms? If we could get enough aid from you the war would be over in a few weeks.'

Inside Afghanistan co-operation is growing between the fighting groups of different parties. The leaders, of very different political allegiances, are trying to align their efforts. Someone says, 'Mahsud is slowly imposing unity over the whole central area of Afghanistan.'

Inside the parties in Peshawar more and more people, some highly placed, dislike their sectarianism, their arrogance, are trying to break down barriers: co-operation between the men who are actually fighting is strengthening both in and outside Afghanistan.

We had certainly not forgotten that we had wanted to find out about the female warriors of Afghanistan: but the atmosphere of some interviews made it impossible to raise the subject. This was not our only problem. Nearly all our interviews suffered from a difference of interpretation of the word 'interview'. For us, an interview is when questions are put, and answered. We had to sit through long exhortations before we could ask questions. This was because of their feelings of isolation, of helplessness – 'As if', one commander put it, 'we cry to you for help, but the wind blows away our words.'

My notes for a certain interview read: 'X is still talking – he began ten minutes ago'. 'Fifteen minutes later, on – on – on – and on'. 'Half an hour has passed'. 'Forty minutes on – he is still talking!' 'At last!'

All these desperate, heart-breaking pleas can be summarized:

1. The war is going well for the muhjahidin, not badly: we, the West, are misinformed.

2. That they intend to go on fighting until they win.

3. Why does the West not help them? Where are the ground-to-air missiles?

4. They need food: the Russians are burning their crops, destroying their fields, their irrigation systems.

We are spending hours and hours in smoky hotel rooms, in rooms in party offices drinking Coca-Cola, and listening to discussions about why the West does not help the muhjahidin. For me the most painful is: 'They obviously don't know how barbarous the Russians are; if they did they would help us.' This takes me back to the old Southern Rhodesia where, year after year, decade after decade, I listened to Africans saying, 'If our brothers in England

70

knew how we were being treated they would help us.' The men who said this were the forerunners of the militants who were soon to come on the stage. These now despise the generation before, calling them 'Uncle Toms', I think unfairly. It is one thing to be part of a great movement where everyone has the same opinions, quite another to be isolated, as most of those men were. They were armed with the knowledge that they were in the right because their land had been stolen from them by the British, but that the people in England had said that their rights, the African rights, must be respected. And so they repeated innocently, and very stubbornly, 'When our brothers in England know— '

Their brothers in England never gave a damn about them. When I came out of Southern Rhodesia and tried to tell people how the whites treated the Blacks in South Africa or in Southern Rhodesia, I, together with half a dozen others who were trying to change public opinion, were called 'Reds', 'Communists', 'Liberals' – always a bad word in Southern Africa – 'troublemakers', and so on. We were patronized, put down, laughed at. A debate on the situation in Southern Rhodesia would empty the House of Commons. Criticism of South Africa was just beginning in certain limited quarters. This was partly due to certain novels that were being written: one was Alan Paton's *Cry the Beloved Country*. But Southern Rhodesia, a British colony? – of course we couldn't behave badly! *What! We, the British?* But I do wonder more and more: suppose people had been prepared to listen then in the early 1950s, to the few voices who were shouting warnings, – would later disasters have been prevented? The seven years' long civil war in Southern Rhodesia for example? In my view, yes. A decade later it became what is tellingly called 'received opinion' to criticize the white regimes in South Africa, but by then it was too late.

'*If people in the West knew how we in Afghanistan are suffering—* ' Not all the diagnoses of western motives are so innocent.

'The United States and the Soviet Union have a secret understanding: Russia can do what it likes with us in Afghanistan provided they lay off South America. That accounts for Grenada, the Soviet Union stepped over that line and had to be punished; it was not in keeping with this secret agreement.' This was from a certain muhjahid wearing a Russian fur cap that he had taken off a Russian soldier he had killed two weeks ago up near Kabul.

A muhjahid with scars from many battles and fingers blown off by a 'toy' bomb. 'It suits the Americans that we keep the Russians bogged down here in Afghanistan. While we keep them busy they will think twice about starting something else. Our struggle keeps the balance of power. Suppose we threw the Russians out of Afghanistan tomorrow? Then they would be free to start some little adventure somewhere else. Perhaps some fighting on the Chinese border, perhaps a little excursion into Europe. Europe is like the United States, you are divided and that makes you vulnerable. Sweden perhaps? Sweden is soft because it has been neutral for so long. When the Russian Bear attacked Finland it was badly mauled and they saw how the Norwegians fought the Germans.'

Here is a muhjahid speaking in the Hiriquat office: 'It is obvious that America could end this war now if they gave us enough aid, yet they do not do it; why not? America is

72

still transfixed by Vietnam, something in them says, If this little country of Afghanistan, so much worse armed than the Vietnamese, can beat the great Russian nation, then we (the Americans) are worse even than the Russians. This is one strand of their thinking and perhaps they are not conscious of it. This is why they deliberately keep the war at a low level; they don't want the Russians to win in Afghanistan, but they don't want us to win either. When we win, it will be the first time a war has been won against Communism and it will be won by a parcel of ragged muhjahidin, and this will make America look bad. The basic trouble is that the United States is divided, but the Russians are not at all divided, they are a world imperialist power and they know exactly what they want and how to get it. They achieve their results by oppression and lies.'

A group of muhjahidin sit on the hotel lawn under the trees, nine of them. They are from another party, not Hiriquat. Again I am impressed by the very different faces: they are from different parts of Afghanistan. An Afghan has explained: 'Afghanistan is a mix of different peoples with different origins. They don't necessarily like each other. But they leave each other alone. It is not unlike the Scots, the Welsh, the English. You don't like each other all that much, but you don't fight each other. The nomads – like the Kochis, the Mongols, the Turkomen, the Kirghiz, the Uzbeks, and so on and so on – they see themselves as different peoples, but they unite to fight an invader.'

This lot had just come from fighting near Kabul. They were obviously battle-weary.

Just before they arrived we had been discussing the *Guardian* newspaper which had published three articles by a journalist, Jonathan Steele, who had been a Russian guest and had swallowed everything they had told him. He had even fallen for the Potemkin Village trick, which the Russians have been using successfully for centuries. (Potemkin was the general under Catherine the Great, her favourite lover, who used to build the façades of prosperous villages to conceal the squalid poverty along the routes the court, or foreigners, were to travel. The Russians these days show gullible journalists a still undamaged area, saying that it is such and such an area, in fact bombed, destroyed, that the journalists have asked about.)

Was it not surprising the the *Guardian* should take a pro-Soviet position? Not at all, I had said: the *Guardian* has always been liable to lapses. At the time of the Central African Federation (now forgotten, but at the time a prominent issue) which was a last-ditch attempt by the whites to preserve their position by amalgamating Southern Rhodesia, Northern Rhodesia and Nyasaland (now Zimbabwe, Zambia and Malawi), the *Guardian* was an enthusiastic supporter of the idea, together with newspapers from whom you would expect such an attitude.

It gave me a strong feeling of improbability to hear the *Guardian* mentioned in such surroundings, together with other western newspapers.

Said a muhjahid: 'Why are you surprised? The British invaded half the world on the argument that it was their right to "civilize" people. They tried it on us. Now the British have lost their Empire but they haven't stopped being imperialists. When the Russians invade and destroy they call it "civilizing" and "modernizing". Just as the European imperialist powers did. That is why newspapers like the *Guardian* support the Russians: they can't be imperialists themselves any longer, but they can support imperialist attitudes at second hand, through the Russians.'

An interview with the Minister of Education in Hiriquat began with the usual appeal for aid and a statement of their heroic stance. Then he said: 'If we win tomorrow, we will have enough people to run Afghanistan well, there is so much talent, skill and expertise going to waste among the refugees in the camps and among the muhjahidin. But if we don't win this war for ten years then we will suffer badly because our children are not getting a modern technological education. Yes, some of our children are being helped but not enough, there is a very great deal of talent going to waste. The Pakistanis help with our children but they are not able to help us as much as they would like because they are also suffering: it is not a rich country. All the parties in Peshawar and Quetta have schools but again not enough, none of us has enough money to pay teachers properly. The parents in the camps try to help but they have no money. That is one problem: the problem of education in the refugee camps. Remember there are very many children in the refugee camps. Most families have between four and ten children, and they are not being educated. The Liberated Areas of Afghanistan are another problem. We do have elementary networks of schools on the old pattern: mosque schools, religious schools and others, but we have no advanced schools. If we built a secondary school the Russians would at once bomb it. The Russians always bomb schools and hospitals. They are logical, they do not wish us to have an educated population, they do not wish the muhjahidin to recover when they are wounded: that is why they bomb schools and hospitals. Now something good is happening; the USA has said that if the parties here in Peshawar collaborate, they will give us some money to establish more schools in the Liberated Areas.'

We asked, 'Do you agree with this, that the parties should all agree to collaborate?'

'Certainly we in this party agree: in the Liberated Areas children of all parties are accepted in our schools – the Hiriquat schools. It is a very good thing that the Americans make this condition. But the aid they are giving is not enough. Now if other countries could send us as much for our education as America is doing, we would perhaps begin to see the end of our difficulties.'

A refugee has to be registered with one of the parties to get food rations. This means people who are not members of a party are unregistered and starve, or have to be fed by relatives who are already on short rations. To spell it out: some of the most independent-minded people who do not want to be defined by a party can starve, or have an extremely difficult time keeping themselves and their children fed.

Not all these refugees are in the camps; we spent a couple of days visiting people who had found a niche for themselves in Peshawar itself. They build warrens of little mud homes for themselves on an empty lot, or fit themselves in somehow into existing streets.

At once began the tangles of problems which old hands take for granted – and even seem to enjoy – as the inevitable part of 'The Peshawar Experience'. Since the warrior women of Afghanistan, or even news of them, continued to evade us, we decided to film and interview educated women. A certain young man had been assigned to us by a party, to look after us, show us everything. (He had been a muhjahid, had been sent out of the fighting to look after relatives in the camps.) He said there was no problem at all about any of us, even Leon, filming these women. And we set off to the streets in question in his company. When we got there, we all took our shoes off and sat exchanging courtesies with several men, and then we three women were taken through to the women's quarters. These were two little rooms and a little courtyard, everything poor, clean, spare. They were furnished in the Afghan style with cushions or mattresses around the walls, matting on the floor. The walls were of whitewashed plaster and brick. There were two young women and an old woman and many children, all friendly, crowding around, anxious to talk. You always have problems talking with the muhjahidin because it is their convention to present themselves as intrepid and heroic, but with women there are no such problems. They tell you at once what it was like, how terrible, how frightening, how they suffered, how they suffer now. They weep; they tell you all the details that journalists long to hear and which it is so hard to get from the men.

This family came down through the mountains four years ago. Their village, full of women and children, was bombed by the Russians: the men had gone off to fight. 'There was nothing left of our village,' they said. 'In our family we kept our stores in a cellar under the house. We went down there and were saved, though the house was bombed over us. There were a hundred people in the group that came out of the village and seven from our family, including this child here.' (A bright little girl, now nine, Nadala, says she remembers everything of that terrible journey.) 'There was snow and there was ice, no water, our children's tongues were swollen from lack of water. It took us two weeks, the Russians bombed us all the way, they dive bombed us day and night. This girl here' – one of the young women – 'was on a horse with a baby under her arm, the Russian aeroplane came low and she felt blood running; it was from the baby. She fell off the horse, the baby was dead. Many had their feet frozen from frostbite. Of the hundred who left with us only ten got through the mountains to Pakistan. Now we live here in this place. The men came after us, it was some weeks later. Then, when they knew that we were all right, they went back to fight with the muhjahidin.'

It was the old woman who did the talking; crying, laughing, miming the sound of the diving planes, the tanks, gunfire, shells. She was full of life, and anger. We all sat there close together, we women with the children, and understood each other very well, getting on the way women do. We did have a Farsi speaker among us, but we would have done quite well without.

Enough time having been allotted to politeness, we asked if we could film them. At once there was reluctance, uneasiness. The two young women said their husbands were not there and it was they who had to give permission. One was obviously frightened of her husband. The bad moment passed and the chat went on. They were complaining about the narrowness of their lives now, shut up all together after their spacious life in the village.

Then, all at once two men, the husbands, appeared and

everything changed. One of them was a schoolteacher speaking some English. He had been fighting in the Afghan Army until very recently, but he had deserted with four thousand soldiers, taking their Kalashnikovs and six tanks with them. Hundreds of these men came to Peshawar. The other was a man who became for us a symbol of the frustrations of Peshawar, even of 'The Peshawar Experience' itself. He was a shorter man than most Afghans, slighter, with a tight gloomy look, suspicious, a bully. He was the feared husband. And suddenly the women had vanished off the verandah and were inside, looking out through windows, or cooking in a tiny cubbyhole of a kitchen, holding a veil over their faces; well in the background. The two men had taken their places, sitting on the verandah near us with the children on their laps and shoulders; obviously they were very good fathers. The two young women were both pregnant; both were nursing small babies, and there were older children. These women, Afghan beauties, all swollen and milky and hung about with infants, were vulnerable, needing defence: it was easy to see them through the men's eyes. We were looking at a stage of family life long gone in the West, blown into the past by birth control and Women's Liberation. This possessive, angry, jailer husband with his hot eyes was probably as good a husband as he was a father, in the old style: uxorial, jealous, sexual, demanding, all-encompassing.

Some of us emancipated women have weak moments when we dream of – well, this is what we dream of: a real, old-fashioned husband. Unfortunately you can't have one thing without the other: you can't have your cake and eat it. The friendly companionable men of our style, and life,

are not ever going to be anything like this uxorial policeman (he was really a policeman, in Security) whose wife
was afraid of him. Such men never surround their women
with fierce, angry, hungry need: and if they do, they are
not allowed to get away with it for long. 'Who do you think
you are, Hitler?' And so they are uncertain, and easily drift
away. They have never been really engaged, not in their
deepest instincts. What I was watching there on that little
verandah was an extreme away from western women's
experience: the passionate, sexual husband; and the more
children, the better.

But it was like looking into a small, hot prison.

While I was having these thoughts – all of them would
have been considered barmy by both the male and female
Afghans there – the men were holding forth about Jihad
and about the Russians. Did we realize that the Russians
had killed at least a million civilians? They thought the
number was much larger. Did we realize that the women
and children we were looking at might just as well have
been dead? Did we know that there were at least three
million refugees here in Pakistan but probably nearer four
million? What about the million, probably two million,
refugees in Iran? Did we realize— ?

If we could not film the young women, perhaps we
could the old woman? Why not? – they conceded gener-
ously.

And then we began explaining publicity – 'the image' –
propaganda – information. These people did not understand anything about this, it is foreign to them.

'Why do you want us to say it again, we've just told
you?', asked the old woman reasonably.

'We want to show you telling your story to people in

America because they don't understand what has happened to you.'

'The Russians bombed our village and then we came over the mountains and— ' But she is speaking mechanically now.

Suddenly one of us asked, 'Tell us about your home in Afghanistan.'

And now the old woman bursts into tears, forgetting all about the camera, and begins a plaint or a chant like this: 'Oh, Afghanistan, Afghanistan is my sweetheart, I long for my home, for my homeland, for my people, for my Afghanistan.' I think of the irony that of all the people in the world the Russians ought to understand this, 'I long for my homeland' – for they never stop going on about their homeland, their *rodina*.

The teacher pushes forward a little boy, who has a rough Kalashnikov made of wood. He shoots with it 'd-d-d-d-d-!' and shouts 'Freedom and death!' when his father directs him with 'Freedom or death!'

'As long as there are Russians we shall fight,' say the men and the old woman and the children, just in case we hadn't got the point.

Leon never got in to film this family. Meanwhile he was talking in the outer room with two young men who had been students in Kabul but who cannot get places in university in Pakistan. 'We have plenty of time now, we are free, as you can see,' they say, laughing. They are the brothers of a young woman doctor who works in a clinic that treats refugee women and children. She supports everyone in the family. And what happened to the young man who had said there would be 'no problem' about filming women? He disappeared somewhere.

81

We, the women, go into the doctor's room. It reminds me of times in my life when I have been poor. It is a bare whitewashed room with cheap, pretty, coloured mats on the floor, pictures torn from magazines on the walls, and a bright bedspread. Around the walls are mattresses and pallets on which we sit, everyone but me comfortably cross legged. I don't know how they do it. It is a hot, humid room. Her father had run a factory for woollen goods in Kabul, and he was secretly helping the muhjahidin. The servants heard the Communists planning to take him to prison and they came to warn him. He fled with his family, 'And so we came down over the mountains, bombed by the Russians— '

The mother was an accountant, has worked in America. All have seen other countries. The young woman doctor says that she was free in Kabul, wore western dress, studied and worked as she liked. Now she is in Purdah, has to be veiled the moment she shows her face out of doors. She cannot even go to the library to get books: her brothers have to bring her books. She has nothing to do but read in the evenings; 'What else is there for us to do?' It shows how thoroughly I had become affected by the stern, puritanical Pakistan spirit that I had to make myself ask, 'There is no café, or restaurant, or perhaps even a theatre you can go to?' – feeling as if I was asking, 'Do you perhaps frequent brothels?' Her smile acknowledged the ridiculousness of the question and my consciousness of its ridiculousness.

A refugee camp typically consists of a maze of little rooms leading into each other with, sometimes, if they are lucky, little courtyards. The walls are usually of mud, sometimes

82

whitewashed. Or there are hundreds of tents, each surrounded by a low mud wall. The patterns of Purdah insist
that there must be an outer room for the men where the
women may not come if there are men visitors; and this
pattern is maintained when possible. The rooms are
cramped, they have nothing in them but the pallets around
the walls, a few shelves for food and possessions. This is
rock-bottom poverty. There are always a lot of children.
Here the women manage somehow on the meagre rations
doled out through the parties. Their men are fighting and
come to visit when they can.

Sometimes a family or a group of families has a man who
will look after them. Several times we heard that Mahsud,
Hakkani, other commanders, instructed a muhjahid to
leave the fighting and go to care for his family.

These are far from passive recipients of aid and food.
Peshawar is full of Afghans who have started every kind of
little business. In the old markets of Peshawar they are
selling food, Afghan goods of all kinds; hangings, carpets,
brassware, clothes and sad mementoes of the dead Russian
soldiers: their fur hats, caps, their Red Star badges, belts
and so on. These things are brought down from Afghanistan all the time on horses, donkeys, as are letters, and
news from home. A continual traffic goes on. If the
Afghans were less enterprising perhaps the Pakistanis
would be less uneasy? Pakistanis complain that the
Afghans take their jobs. The reply is, 'We are not taking
your jobs, we start our own businesses.' The camps themselves are full of little enterprises.

I listen to two middle-class Afghans, surviving somehow in Peshawar, discuss why the West is reluctant to help
refugees.

'I think it is because we refuse to be helpless,' says one. 'What the West responds to is a starving child – preferably black. But suppose this was put on the television screen: an Afghan fighting with the muhjahidin is wounded, cannot fight any longer. He sells fried dumplings beside a road where the muhjahidin pass on their way to visit their families in the camp. His wife and seven children are in this camp. He earns just enough working from dawn to dusk to keep his children from starving, but they are malnourished, he can't buy them warm clothes, and they don't go to school. Would people respond to this story?'

'No,' says the other. 'It is a question of conditioning. They have been conditioned to respond to the black child, but not to us.'

I asked a Pakistani friend if he thought that in the long run this invasion of Afghan enterprise and energy would benefit Pakistan. Usually, when a country takes in refugees, all kinds of benefits result a generation or two later. He said that Pakistan had too many problems already to benefit from any more. Americans and other people, when put this question, thought that the Pakistanis could do with an infusion of Afghan energy and toughness.

'Three million' – it is easy to say 'Three million, four million refugees' – but it is not until you see the miles and miles of refugee camps that you begin to feel what this might mean – endless little mud rooms or the shacks that replace them; endless swarms of children, most of them not being educated; women cooped up together, no proper sanitation; not enough water. And the refugees are still coming in and coming in from Afghanistan in their thousands, their hundreds of thousands. An American doctor said, 'The Russians won't be happy until they've driven out every Afghan from Afghanistan. This is what they want, an empty country to colonize and to exploit without opposition. They know that as long as there are Afghans alive inside the country they will have to fight them.'

'Yes, but as long as there are any Afghans outside the country they will have to fight them.'

'And that is why they are trying to get the borders closed.'

Nearly all the traffic back and forth – fighters, their equipment, their animals, goods for the markets, journalists, spies and villagers; – goes through the lands of the Pushtuns. These have never paid allegiance to any government. They do not love Pakistan, or Kabul, or the Russians. They have a long and surprising history; they are, they claim, Beni Israel of the ten tribes of Israel, brought to Afghanistan long, long ago by Nebuchadnezzar. They are, in short, Jews. They have Old Testament names; there are Hebrew inscriptions on old grave stones; they pursue some Jewish customs. These people are famed as wild and intransigent even among the Afghans. They have refused to co-operate with the Russians in destroying the muhjahidin; but now the Russians are using a very clever policy to win them over. The Pushtuns believe that land has been stolen from them, they feel themselves pressed into a small area. The Russians offer them land if they will move away from the border areas, or, if they stay, give money to them to refuse aid to the muhjahidin. These pressures are working – to an extent. Will they succeed? If so, one of the roads into Afghanistan from Pakistan will be closed to the muhjahidin – perhaps the most important one. But the Pushtuns do not stay bribed, as history shows – they have always taken money from wherever it is offered and then pursued their own interests. They hate the Russians and that is the muhjahidin's hope.

Four of us returned to the quarter where the unregistered Afghans live, escorted by our little policeman, who made it clear we could not go there without him. By what right? Who had said so? We were never to find out. Some kind of a mentor we were bound to have – said the experienced. We might think we were quite unremarkable; three women, British (from old Southern Rhodesia and born in Iran, but let that pass); a Texan; an Afghan girl born in Britain; and a Swedish film maker – nothing out of the ordinary in the West where people mix and mingle, move around all the time – but as far as the Authorities were concerned we were quite impossible. What were we doing? Well, we said, working for Afghan Relief and looking at – But why together? Well we're friends, we said. *But, but but!* – 'You had much better put up with your policeman, he's not as bad as you think and you might get much worse.'

Every little alleyway, every little dusty space, every house has running down its sides a shallow ditch with water in it, and sewage, anything that a house needs to lose. The smell is strong. Nancy Sheils, used to Southern India, says that modern sewage disposal is a western superstition and that billions of people manage perfectly well without it. I say that before we in Britain got our sewage systems, people died of cholera, typhoid, dysentery, and I was not prepared to be argued into tolerance of gutters full of turds. But I did notice that on my second visit to the area I hardly noticed what had absorbed my attention on the first.

Close to the other rooms we visited, crammed with people of all ages, lived a Qazi and his family. He was something like a magistrate, but here he works as a janitor. One of the women, his sister-in-law, is a relative of the Daud who invited the Russians into Afghanistan. We did not like to ask her what she now thinks of her distinguished relative. Young women, old women, children, and the Qazi, some speaking English, were keen to keep us there, desperate for any kind of sociability in this boring routine of theirs in the crammed room, in this warren of streets. And the women, of course afflicted by Purdah.

These are people who had had houses, gardens, the good life, in Afghanistan.

Then we were taken, without warning, to a dusty space between three brick walls where a tent had been stretched. In the tent was a young woman, her face covered of course, a man who looked sullen and ill with desperation, a boy of about five or six, who was hanging about with nothing to do. There was a baby wrapped like a papoose in mosquito netting, just waking from sleep, looking quite healthy and normal. But a baby had died 'as we came down through the mountains', and another child, a year older than the baby but the same size, lay face down and so still and heavy that we thought it was dead or dying. There was something very wrong with it. The family was not registered for food: the man earned a few rupees a week as a kind of porter in the market. Now it was hot, muggy, dusty in this tent. Soon it would be cold and dusty, but that is where they would be throughout the winter. Where they are now.

All the lanes we walked through were full of Afghans standing about talking. All this area was full of Afghans. Stalls sold fruit and vegetables. Most of the men were muhjahidin visiting between battles. Then we were taken to a room which I was thinking of as luxurious, until I realized how my standards had shifted in a couple of days. It was a decent sized room with a high ceiling, and the walls were clean white. On the floor was a real Afghan carpet. Around the walls the mattresses had on them rugs and cushions, and the bed a woven, many-coloured cover. A fan revolved in the ceiling. Above all there was a re-frigerator in the corner of the room, the first I had seen. Then I realized in Britain, certainly in America, this machine would be considered too ancient even for a poor, second-hand shop. This was the best room we saw: the people living in it were teachers and had work.

A commander from Paghman visited us several times; he is from yet another party and small fry compared to the man who orchestrates whole campaigns. He was a peasant's son. Then, being clever, was in the regular army, where he distinguished himself before The Cata-strophe. He now has a few hundred men under him. The first night he had just come from the battles in Paghman and he was high, garrulous, restless, boastful. Next day, adrenalin spent, he had become sober and was very tired, he said he was suffering from 'battle shock'; he could not sleep because he saw Russians all night in his mind's eye and he had to stay awake to kill them. He has been fighting Russians for seven years. Three days before, eighty Russians were killed with eight hundred wounded. The Russians have been trying to get Paghman for seven years. It was once the 'Paradise of Afghanistan', full of orchards, gardens, fields, villages, irrigation systems, with half a million people living there. Now it is a desert; you'd never know that there were once gardens and all that water and the flowers. The Russian bombs have gone so deep that the water table thirty feet down has been punctured. In parts the ground has been made sour and spoiled. The big castle at Paghman still guards the entrance to the valley. This was the strong-point from which they attacked Kabul in the old days. Now the Russians control five kilometres around Kabul and that only by day. 'It is we,' he says, 'who decide what happens outside and inside Kabul. For instance, last May Day the Russians announced a celebration, you know, their International Worker celebration, and we decided to join in. We positioned two lots of men near the castle where there was a narrow defile and we lay in wait near a Russian post. We knew two military convoys were coming through, we had been told so by our informers. We did not get our chance until four o'clock, then we cut the convoys into several parts. Our men descended on the convoys; we even used hatchets and iron bars, because the Russians can't stand up to that kind of fighting. We captured Kalashnikovs and DSHKs and armoured personnel carriers. There was no place to take all that stuff, so we poured petrol over the lot and set fire to it; the explosions were seen all over Kabul. That was our contribution to their May Day. It was a very famous attack, you can check it if you like. I say this because they accuse us of exaggeration. It is not true, there are battles all the time that no one hears about, except for the Russians, and they know very well we don't exaggerate.'

On another visit, with yet another selection of men, he said, 'The Russian methods are inconsistent with their political pretensions. Early on, some people fell for all that fine talk but that was a long time ago. We think now that there might be two thousand Communists in the whole country and some of them are pretending, they have to. The Russians give jobs to people who will obey them, who they are sure of, or who they think they can be sure of. This is classical imperialism. They then make deals with the relatives of the people working for them or they take them prisoner and threaten to torture them if the people they employ don't play ball with them. This creates opportunities for the Resistance. These people can often be counted on to work carelessly or to shut their eyes to something, to take a risk. Effectively, there are no real collaborationists. They have learnt from the Russians, who are corrupt, how to outwit their system and they are much more useful where they are than if they had fled. The very first thing the Russians do is to create a network of collaborators. Another method inconsistent with their pretensions: instead of collectivizing land, as they claim to do, they have created a large number of petty capitalists. If someone has fifty acres, the Russians take forty and they leave the man with ten. Then they say, 'If you behave and don't collaborate with the muhjahidin, you can keep your ten acres.' With the other forty acres they get four more little capitalists, controlled in the same way. Another policy is used in towns. If someone has fifty thousand Afghanis, they allow him ten thousand and take forty thousand and give this to people who will spy for them. They aim to make their control of our country self-financing. When they go into a town they mark out the good houses, evict the owners and hand over these homes to their stooges; aiming to create a subservient elite. But we know who the real stooges are, and they do not. We have so many people working for us inside their network that we always know what they are doing and what they are planning. That is why people with so few arms and so little ammunition can do so well.' This man talked with great admiration of Mahsud, who is from a different party: 'Mahsud has captured the emerald mines back from the Russians. His agents are buying arms in the international markets, he already has eighteen helicopters and thirteen jet planes taken from the Russians repaired and fit for use, he has six hundred tanks – he will have more by now. He has somewhere to keep them, but when we captured sixty tanks near Paghman castle we had to burn them.' (The mountains are full of hiding places; caves and natural fortresses, which the muhjahidin commanders use as headquarters. Not only the muhjahidin. An army of Turkomen is still fighting the Russians decades after the conquest of their country. They had 'a city of reeds' in a reed forest near the Russian border, where they had an army, arms, even hospitals and libraries. They have moved this HQ now to somewhere else.)

This commander said the KHAD were out to get him but he was not allowed to carry a gun in Pakistan to protect himself; 'The KGB have influence here where you wouldn't expect it, that is why I'm not allowed a gun.'

While these visits were going on we, the five of us, were in Deans Hotel, which must be the only one of its kind in the world. It was built under the Raj and consists of single storey buildings scattered over a large area among gardens, trees. The rooms are stuffy and hot, but when I woke in the night I was freezing cold: the sweat had dried on me because of the blast from the labouring fan.

Then I could not sleep again because of the noise. The air conditioning roared. The fans whirred. The machinery of the air conditioning thudded and banged. It seemed as if this block of rooms was a ship chuntering along a river, chug-chug, chug-chug. With everything in movement, curtains, the edges of chair covers, clothing billowing on the back of a chair, the illusion was strengthened. If I looked out of the window I would see meandering water, jungle trees. The space above our line of five rooms was empty, presumably attics. Astonishing noises came from there, much too loud for rats. Birds had colonized, or even small animals. The feeling of being accompanied, even watched, was strong. When I looked up at a certain crack I expected to see eyes, and they need not have been animal. But when I did actually look out of the window, these fancies vanished: only shadowy lawns, trees, shrubs, dim stars, bedroom blocks where all was dark – and the night watchman on his rounds.

I don't want to knock this unique hotel for fear they will pull it down and put up some flavourless international monstrosity. The atmosphere can be conveyed by this small tale: as usual, unable to sleep because of the stuffiness, I was walking around in my room at four a.m., when I heard a loud bang. A gun shot? The place is used by armament sellers, drugs dealers, crooks, spies, desperadoes of all kinds, as well as journalists, aid workers and ordinary tourists. I did nothing about this immediately, but after five minutes looked out: no one on the verandah or in the gardens, it was all quiet and innocent, and the windows of the block of bedrooms at right angles to ours were dark. Shortly afterwards there were some knocks on my door. Again I did not go to the door and when I did there was nothing at all to be seen. Half an hour later a series of sounds, which it is tempting to try and define. They were not the type of sound you'd expect at four-thirty a.m. in a respectable hotel, let's say, in Tunbridge

Wells. Voices? – no. More like something heavy being pushed about or dragged. I stood watching: nothing to be seen. Slowly the morning came. Two muhjahidin emerged out of a bedroom near us. They threw their blankets over their shoulders and strolled off into the dawn. The hotel watchmen went to the gate with them. From this series of little events any number of tales could be concocted.

It goes without saying that in the hotels all the taxi drivers who wait for customers outside the hotel, the waiters, the man behind the desk in reception, are police agents.

About three days after arrival you realize you have become suspicious in a way that in any other place would be laughable. The first thought about anybody is: 'In whose pay are you?' Paranoia? Nonsense! – essential survival kit.

The whole place is full of intrigue, mysterious happenings, spies. Characters so obviously suspect that a novelist could only put them into satire, or a skit, approach with a parade of innocence to ask questions of casual cunning, and to explain why they are in Pakistan or Peshawar, and why they have felt impelled to visit you in your room, or to join you at the table. You want to laugh out loud; you want to catch their eye so they laugh too. . . But no, the rules of the game forbid it: solemnity prevails. Then they disappear, presumably to file their report for someone or other. This is an essential part of 'The Peshawar Experience', and means you have been given a taste of a seedy, dangerous, black comedy that I am sure nowhere else can match.

I have to report that while the Afghan situation is easily understood, tragic and complicated though it may be, I couldn't make any sense of Pakistan, which seems a mass of contradictions. The four English-language newspapers we read every morning while we ate breakfast under the trees, watched by hotel cats, crows and what seemed to be some variety of vulture, depict a country full of riots and crisis. Every issue has despairing articles about the state of the nation, but what we read in the newspapers was not mirrored in the people we met or in the life we experienced. The characteristic of the Pakistanis seems imperturbable, good-natured indolence. Charm. They are a charming lot. Charm oozes from friendly brown eyes, smiles, faces. Charm is the quality that eases the way in a thousand transactions that otherwise would not go forward at all. When you think that there is no hope of that permit, that plane ticket, that appointment, charm comes to the rescue: infinite reserves of good nature. A nation of charmers! How is this possible? Enquiries from Pakistani friends in England when I got back elicited cynical remarks, but I prefer to remain unenlightened. After all, I did not go there to study Pakistan.

I did however ask about Miss Bhutto everywhere I went. You might think that in a nation where the veiling of women is such an issue that someone would say 'She is a woman!' Not at all! 'She's too young,' they say. 'Zia is too much of an old fox for her.' 'She is nothing but a Soviet agent.' 'She will make a good member of the Opposition when she's had more experience.' But never, 'She is a woman.'

We had plenty of time to loaf around under the trees or to sit out at night on the lawns looking at the moon. We sat around. We sat. We sat. That is because of the way things

94

go along in Pakistan, slowly, unpredictably, infuriatingly.
Appointments are made – are not broken but simply do
not happen. People do not turn up at the time set, or at all.
Complicated sequences of events planned in the western
manner, which means in every confidence that they will
happen, do not even begin. We were already, after three or
four days, saying every evening: 'And what do we *imagine*
is going to happen tomorrow?' All the old hands we met,
the western doctors training Afghans, the people working
in the hospitals, the aid workers, had acquired a defensive
watchful humour, recognizably a defence against hysteria:
'You see, the bureaucracy here is— '

I would not like to have to deal with it for long myself.

Perhaps the thing that frustrated us most was the difficulty of getting the men to talk in as much colourful
detail as the women. This pinpoints a difference between
them and us which is not necessarily flattering to us, for
whom everything has to be personalized. I have here notes
of a conversation with a certain muhjahid commander. We
had all been talking all afternoon about – of course – why
the West does not help them; about the Russians, about
the different national characteristics of various western
countries. (For instance the French – hysterical and emo-
tional, though they have done a great deal to help us;
Americans – traders, but without any long-term understanding of their real interests; the British – part imperial,
part traders; the Swedes – very sincere and hard working;
the Russians – all imperialists.) In the middle of the
familiar discourse about the arrogance of the mullahs he
said something which indicated that he'd had an extraordinary personal history. This conversation then ensued.

'You say you simply left the Afghan Army to join the

muhjahidin?'

'Yes.'

'But how did it happen?'

'Well, it wasn't easy to choose the right time to leave with them watching us all the time, so we left when we could.'

'Yes, but what *exactly* happened?'

'We took some tanks and we left.'

'You must understand that people in the West will be fascinated to hear this story.'

'But we keep telling you! Tell them that large numbers of Afghans leave the Afghan Army to fight with the muh-jahidin.'

'Yes, yes, I know but tell us, please, exactly what happened.'

'What do you want to know?'

'Was it night time when you left?'

'What? Yes, of course it was night. We fight at night, so the Russians have to too. We say if we don't feel like sleeping tonight then the Russians will have to stay awake too.'

'And on that particular night?'

'We had sent a messenger to the muhjahidin saying we wanted to join them. There was going to be an attack on their positions, and we told them this. They sent a message back saying that we should pretend to attack and then join them, so that's what we did.'

'You make it sound very easy.'

'It was easy, because we planned it.'

'Did anybody get killed?'

'Yes, many Russians, not so many of us.'

'When you say you sent messages to the muhjahidin and

they sent messages to you, how did this happen?'

'There are so many people in the Afghan Army working for the muhjahidin we always know what they are doing and they know what we're doing.'

'You say that some of you were killed?'

'Yes.'

'Was anyone wounded?'

'I got a wound in my arm. The man next to me was killed.'

'And then?'

'I came to a muhjahidin hospital in Peshawar and after a few weeks I went back to fight with the muhjahidin near Kabul.'

Some people leave Peshawar feeling they have escaped from A Night in Casablanca. As for me, I was grateful to escape with my life from the traffic. Brought up in Rhodesia, where speed limits or traffic regulations were regarded as an attack on personal liberty, I thought I'd seen everything. After sunset, a million bicycles, none with lights, crammed the roads. Salisbury got its first traffic lights (to the accompaniment of sarcastic cheers) at the end of World War Two. Peshawar's traffic is like a Paris rush hour but four times as bad, and complicated with horse carts, donkey carts, bullocks and cows wandering across the road. Bicycles, perhaps with several people on them, are often without lights. There are cars of all kinds, and the buses of the region like enormous tin cans decorated with slogans, pictures of film stars, quotations from the Koran. There are, as well, the peculiar contributions of the subcontinent to international mobility; motorcycles converted into miniature taxis which should not, but do, carry up to five people and jolt your bones to jelly. Everyone drives on the horn, apparently relying on sound and not on sight. The shortest journey is a series of near-fatalities, 'But you acquire a sixth sense,' says a Pakistani friend happily, swerving and careering everywhere, under the noses of beasts and machines. One simply had to decide not to look: better to meet death unprepared. In every city you feel enclosed by what it characteristically is; and after a few days in Peshawar I felt that all the world was a dangerous net of streets, hazy with fumes and dust – dust everywhere, mixed with the smell of petrol and diesel, filling your nostrils, gritty on your skin and in your hair.

In the gardens of Dean's Hotel the dusty traffic was on the other side of hedges which, however, did not keep out the din. The smog dimmed the stars: only the brightest stars could shine through it, for this was not the low, crowding brilliance you expect from a southern night sky which, as soon as the sun goes down, makes human affairs insignificant. On the contrary, humanity imposes itself upwards from the dusty lights of the town: red and yellow spurt low in the dim sky and you think 'Fireworks', but realize that star shells are going up from the Parachinar Valley, where there must be some sort of 'incident' in progress. You sit waiting to see if there are any more star shells, or for the sound of gunfire. Dusty stars, dust on the shrubs and on the verandahs: dust from the cars sweeping in and out of the hotel; dusty sweat which needs several showers a day to wash off.

A dusty landscape, a landscape of earth, was what I'd seen coming in to land and here it was all round me.

But that was before I'd walked in the place – after a few

days of this sitting about and waiting, with intervals of rushing about, which is what our trip had become, I knew I had to walk. I and Nancy Sheils, also a walker, had a rendezvous for five-thirty a.m. and we went along still deserted roads. This enabled us to see how many trees there were everywhere. But it was a wrong direction. Finding ourselves marching along beside a wide malodorous ditch, we gave up, but next morning went the other way and were in the Cantonments, built by the British for their army personnel and, of course, with not a sewage ditch in sight. Where then does the sewage get to? Much better not ask. Here it was all pleasant villas with gardens and courtyards, made for drinking tea and sitting and sitting; and when we visited inside one, I was picturing the British family, similar to mine. The matron like my mother, coping briskly with dust, the heat, the flies and, of course, the lack of proper sanitation. About Kermanshah, where I was born, she would say, 'The servants threw the slops out in the early morning and by midday they were completely dry, you couldn't see where they had been.' Where they were, of course, was blowing all round the landscape in the dust. Easy to imagine how these wives, their tour of duty over, spoke of Peshawar; half-relieved that the hot, lonely dusty struggle was over, half tantalized still by the life that they had not let themselves be part of; the real lives of their servants and of the soldiers their husbands were responsible for. For of course they would have had contact only with these in an official way, never with the families, never with an ordinary Indian. (This was not Pakistan then, it was still India.) In the villa in the Cantonments where we had tea there was a large shadowy living room full of photographs, dominated by

99

the slowly revolving fan: on the wall was a tiger skin – a famous man-eater of whose killing we were told in detail. Rugs from Pakistan and Afghanistan; all kinds of ornaments, lace hangings. It was the combination of the exotic, and the homely British influence, that inspires a hundred thousand Indian restaurants all over Britain. There was a servant, male, watchful, in charge of everything, handing cakes and more cakes, and chips with tomato sauce and delicious sliced fruit and his sharp chiding eye made me remember my mother, laughing; 'And I had to mind my Ps and Qs with the house servants, I can tell you! If I stepped out of line they'd soon let you know it. I had to learn to stand up to them.' These villas are now owned by better-off Pakistanis but the ghosts of the Raj still walk. Our host had been in the British Army in two world wars. He is still all soldier, follows the news of the fighting in Afghanistan, and criticizes or commends the action. He would like to be there, too. . .

There are suburbs full of attractive houses, trees, gardens: Peshawar is spread widely over the plain, but not densely. Looking for an address, you are one minute in a street full of ornamental gateways to large villas; the next you are in a little field growing corn, and fat goats are scavenging hills of garbage. Turn a corner, and you are in villa-land again.

Never can you forget in Peshawar that buildings are short-lived, like people. It is not only the contrast with ponderous London, where buildings are rooted so deep in the earth and make you think of continuity: in Southern Africa I have seen dozens of little towns, villages, dorps, lying just as shallowly on the surface of the soil, but they don't make you think of impermanence in the same way. There are only a few tall modern buildings in Peshawar, thank God: as hideous there as everywhere else. New buildings tend to copy older ones, so that a just-built school is two or three storeys high and has an airy grace, because of memories of the arches and decorations of the Moghuls. A new building may look attacked by time because already there is a dark patch on the lower part of a white wall, as if the earth is reaching up to claim her own. Everything, not only the pathetic mud warrens of the refugees, looks as if it is makeshift, transitory, just put up or just about to fall apart back into the soil. That is the charm of the place, the fascination: 'Dust thou art, and to dust shalt thou return', says this landscape, the ecologist's, the conservationist's paradise.

We were driven out to visit the family of a muhjahid commander who had become our friend. The route was at first through the ordinary streets of Peshawar, lined with these light, graceful, brick or mud buildings, freshly whitewashed or not, sometimes stained or flaking or cracked. The big markets in Peshawar are everything you would expect a medieval oriental market to be: mazes of little lanes and courts and booths, and the roads running out of Peshawar have these same little shops all along them: They are built of mud, or mixed mud and chaff. They have every kind of roof: reeds, old branches, yellow maize plants piled up into a thatch or heaped on reed or pole rafters, and some have mounds of pale gritty earth, and from this soil weeds and grass are growing. The booths sell fruit, vegetables, meat, every kind of manufactured goods; and the men, many of them Afghan, sit in the doorways watching the world go by, or perhaps lie on beds made of string and poles put outside the booths. Sometimes friends join them and then these groups of men sit and gossip and stare at the cars and the traffic, the murderous traffic of Peshawar. But soon the sides of the road swarm with muhjahidin and many of them now are armed because Peshawar is being left behind. Hundreds of them, then thousands, then it seems that all this mass of people are muhjahidin. Among the men moves an occasional woman. You have to force yourself to notice them: their garb, like their gait, is for invisibility. A woman in a bhurka, interestingly, has a more free, casual walk than one who is veiled. A bhurka covers from head to foot; it fits close around the head with a little grille for the eyes and then flows out around her as she walks. The woman inside is in a different world: she is observing, not seen, really invisible (it goes without saying that this bhurka is used for all kinds of dangerous or shady transactions. The authorities on the frontiers between Pakistan and Afghanistan look at hands and feet: is this a muhjahid or a journalist trying to get in to Afghanistan?) A woman in a veil – that is a cloth thrown across her mouth, leaving only her eyes visible – acquires a scurrying furtive look. It is painful to see a woman you have been talking to, a human being, a person, transformed in this way.

When I was back in London I wrapped my head in a veil covering my mouth and my forehead down to the eyebrows. Only my eyes were showing. I went about the streets like this for a day; I had become invisible. Having taken in with a glance my statement 'I don't want to be looked at' – people's eyes slid over and past me. They do not let their eyes engage with yours. Soon I realized that my eyes were trying to make themselves be noticed: in a

Moslem country they would be emphatically made-up. I realized how, usually in buses, on the Underground, passing someone on a pavement, I rely on my face to convey messages with a smile or a look, but now smiles were invisible, mouth hidden. When a mouth is covered up you become very conscious of it, soon it seems something forbidden, or unpleasant, or shameful, something erotic that must be concealed; even a wound. I began to wonder what sort of oral fixation or obsession had first ordered the covering of the mouth – which is nowhere mentioned in the Koran or by the Prophet. Somewhere in the early history of Islam there must have been an obsessive authoritarian like Saint Paul who imposed himself on Christianity, tormenting and humiliating women with centuries of prohibitions that could never have emanated from Christ. Liberal Moslems say there are plenty of texts in the Koran on which the equality of women can be established for a reform of Islam. For instance; 'Women are the twin halves of men'; 'Paradise is under the feet of your mother'; or 'What is a woman's property must not be taken from her'. It is on this last text that already Moslems are establishing themselves as businesswomen. It helps too that Mohammed's first wife was a successful trader in her own right.

Why do we have to worry about what was said so many centuries ago? Obviously there is something in the mechanism of the human mind that demands it. Once a year Shia Moslems flagellate themselves, reduce themselves to shocked idiocy by self-mutilation because Mohammed's grandsons were murdered in the fifth century (Christian calendar). Some members of our group saw these Shias being brought into hospital covered with blood, badly wounded, having beaten themselves with iron bars and chains, looking (as one of us of Moslem origin said) rather like Christ taken down from the Cross. Christians endlessly squabble about the interpretation of texts in the Old and New Testaments. I recently heard a witty and learned discourse about how the religion according to St Marx could easily be something quite different from what we are now saddled with; it is only a question of choosing different texts.

People like authority figures, though we try to pretend we do not. The older among us may remember how recently the words of St Freud were turned into dogma by certain of his disciples. Luckily, it looks as if this religion has been nipped in the bud.

There is certainly something in women that responds to being made a prisoner. We have recently seen how sections of Moslem women have claimed that they feel 'free' when veiled. Why not? If that's what makes them happy? – they should not impose their choices on others. In Iran gangs of Orthodox women roamed the streets looking for their 'sisters' who had erred by showing a trace of lipstick, or a loose strand of hair. When they found one, they raked their nails across her lips, pulled her hair, slapped and hit her, shouted epithets like 'whore'. It is, alas, not only men who imprison women.

The road was still crammed with the great, glittering, decorated buses, with motorbike taxis, and with cars; but now there were more carts drawn by bullocks and donkeys. And suddenly you are in the middle of a fertile teeming countryside of fields, trees, irrigation ditches, ponds, streams, trees. Every inch is cultivated. Along the edge of the road contented buffalo wallow or graze, or are taken to ponds for a swim by half-naked little boys; the cows are sleek; the donkeys well fed. I saw no neglected or badly treated animals. Yes, there was one, a worn-out donkey in a Peshawar street pulling a cart owned by a desperate-looking muhjahid. Even the hotel cats looked well fed: perhaps this is because the Prophet is on record for loving cats. Soon the road was being made up: women, perfunctorily veiled, carried earth in shallow baskets. For about a mile men sat at intervals, chipping stones with hammers. Each wore protective glasses, giving him a scholarly air; and fingers were protected by shields as if for ink. These scribes sat unhurriedly chipping away in the shade of wickerwork or cloth shields like little sails. Often there were small graveyards full of sharp sticking-up stones looking like teeth sown into the earth. Sometimes the graveyards were for the muhjahidin and were like big ships sailing along the hillside flying a hundred gay little pennants, mostly green.

Slowly this lush landscape changed, it became drier, stonier. The road, still edged with booths, was crowded solid with vehicles, people, beasts. Several times our taxi was brought to a stop, and we were immediately sur-rounded by staring, sometimes grinning men: we were women, unveiled women, Western women. Little boys called out 'Hello, how are you?,' to show that they were learning English in school, and grave, bearded, turbaned men chided them. But they took no notice and ran along the side of the car laughing. Often we saw the Nuristani face, always a shock, for it is western, with a straight, even a snub nose, blue or green eyes, light hair, perhaps freckles. You have to suppress the impulse to call out as to a fellow countryman. There is a theory that the English, the Angles, originated from these parts. Part of a Nuristani tribe wandered, because of pressure of population on the grazing, for hundreds of years before coming to rest in England: well, here you are inclined to believe it. Soon we turned sharply off the main road on to a track and were at once in a desert landscape. It was all red dust, stony, rough with gulleys and ridges and everywhere old buildings were subsiding back to the earth, and the stubs of old huts, hard shiny red protruberances, showed just above the soil. The dust blew everywhere, the blue sky was veiled by dust. There were brickyards – a brick being the form dust makes in its first ascent away from itself. Here and there was a tent, perhaps taking the advantage of a lone tree or bush; a dwelling for an Afghan refugee family. These tents have also taken a step up towards being a house: here a tent can be a roof and the mud walls built up around it two, three, or more feet high. They are red with dust; the few trees are dusty. No green: a herd of cattle are being driven across the red expanse quickly to some grazing that is well out of sight. The fertile landscape is not more than four or five miles away, but it is hard to believe that here. The red dust of the plain stretches away and away, bounded by a line of green that seems to be immediately under the Himalayan foothills: miles of dust, earth, stones.

A low earth wall, miles long, curves away on one side of the plain. Behind it is a muhjahidin encampment belonging to one of the political parties. Groups of muhjahidin wander across the dust expanse, and they disappear behind a wall. Now every one is armed. The long, smooth, red wall with the blue sky beyond, makes me think of parts of Spain – the grandeur of it, the solitariness. But behind that wall armed men swarm, thousands of them. This landscape only seems empty.

Soon we were in a little village of the mud houses the refugees make for themselves, and now began one of the muddles that seem unavoidable. We had been invited to meet the commander and also his family. Again we had been told it was permitted to film his women. But he was not there: his aides did not know what had happened to him; he had not been home for three days. He had gone off into the fighting in the Valley, they thought. His mother and wife were worried about him. He turned up next day apologetic, but not explanatory, about the incident.

The aides knew nothing about filming the family. Again we three women were taken into the women's quarters at the back and the men sat in the room for men visitors.

These women were much better off than most: they had space. A big mud wall enclosed a large yard where three horses were feeding on the maize stalks we had seen carted along the road for fodder. There were chickens. In a niche in the mud wall was a little garden about two yards square, with jasmine and roses. Dry, dusty, but it was a garden. Two young women, the wives of the commander and of his brother, also a commander, were both pregnant, and nursing babies, and each had a larger child as well: six children in all. The older children were playing with a bird in a small string cage that is like a partridge. It is their pet: I think it has a hard time of it. Both girls are beauties of a certain Afghan type: they have heart-shaped faces with wide cheekbones, full sensuous mouths but with a short upper lip showing white teeth. Their large green eyes, frank and direct and candid, are a world away from the dark secretive eyes of their Pakistani neighbours. They walk and hold themselves like mountain women.

There is an old woman in command of everything, sixty years old, the commander's mother. She is formidable.

What we have been told of the surprises of Purdah at once come to life: we have not even sat down before she has flung up her skirt to show her naked stomach. It is swollen. She has a growth. It is not painful, she says, but not operable. She visits a clinic run by the doctors in exile from Kabul, but they have very few medicines.

We had been told by various people familiar with Islam that if a man falls into the category of 'privileged friend' of a family, then he may go in to visit as he likes with the women of the family in Purdah, who have become a kind of sister, unthinkable sexually. They behave as familiarly with him as with their own menfolk, wandering about not only unveiled but even half dressed, and without any self-consciousness.

We asked these young women if Nancy and Saira might film and photograph them; but their husbands were not present to give permission. The old women and the children – yes, that was different.

The two families live in two smallish rooms with a verandah joining them. The walls were of cement, unpainted. Matting covered the floors. There was a great pile of bedding almost to the ceiling in one corner, and the usual mattresses around the walls, covered with bright cloth. The women wore pretty bright dresses, earrings, necklaces, bangles.

This is cheap jewellery, of beads, plastic. When the war began the women of Afghanistan stripped themselves of their good jewellery, anything of value, and gave it to the fighters to buy guns and arms. Pack animals loaded with this jewellery were driven over the mountains to the camps in Pakistan. Women arriving as refugees in the camps were unlikely to have much left: what they had was sold

for food. The bazaars of Peshawar are full of their necklaces, bracelets, earrings. I bought a necklace: twenty-one
complicated copper pendants sewn on to a brocade braid.
It has the intensely private, personal, look and feel of an
article much used. It is made to be worn close around the
throat. Here it ought to be worn on a high-necked, plain
dress – very smart. It lies on a table in my room and seems
to pull my eyes towards it. Don't forget me! – it says.

They kept offering us tea and we refused, for this meant
they had no tea; if they had it would simply have been
brought in. There was little food, few toys for the children.
It was the old woman who did the talking; animated,
vigorous, confident. When her sons go into battle they
leave the children in her care, not their wives'.

Their story begins, of course: 'And then the Russians
bombed us and destroyed our food and we came across the
mountains— ' Their life here, they say, is poor and dull.
At home they had everything, everyone was happy in
Afghanistan before The Catastrophe! Now they never
leave this camp. Where can they go? And they have no
clothes, the children have only what they are wearing now,
little cotton dresses and shirts and pants: the winter is
coming. 'Besides,' says the old woman, 'we all feel safe
here surrounded by our muhjahidin. In Peshawar people
get killed by KHAD, by the Russians.'

And now we again asked about the women fighters. Had
they heard of them, did they exist?

'Oh yes,' said the old woman at once. 'There is one near
Herat.' (She herself comes from Herat, had married her
husband from there.) 'This woman commander is called
Maryam. She was the only child of her father who said 'I
have only one child, no son, and she must go to Jihad.' He

tied his ammunition belt around her and his men accepted her. She is famous. She is as brave as a man. She says: 'When I find a man as brave as I am, I will marry him.' But she is thirty-five years old and of course she cannot marry until we win the war. She is very clever, this woman commander. For instance, once, when she knew the Russians were coming, she made the village people drive cows and chickens across a bridge. The Russian soldiers are badly fed, and she knew they would stop to chase the cows and chickens. When they got out of the tanks, her soldiers killed them all. Another time the Russians came and she said to them, 'Come in, you are our guests, sit down.' They sat down and she and her soldiers poured petrol around the place and set fire to it and the soldiers burned to death. And there is another woman commander in Panjshir, I have heard of her.'

This woman said that two thousand of her tribe were killed in Herat; twenty-six were killed by napalm as they stood in prayer. 'Herat is wearing white,' she said. (This means they are ready to die, when you say someone is wearing white it means they have their shrouds on ready to die.) She says, 'Why does not the world complain about the destruction of Herat? It was so beautiful and now it is rubble. Why do you let the Russians behave like savages? And Paghman is flat too,' she keens, 'there's nothing left of it, it was so beautiful.'

I have to report that sitting there with the women, all so friendly and sociable and gossipy, inside walls that shut out the world, with the big, brave armed men out there in front, I found myself thinking: 'Ah well, why not leave it all to them?' It was exactly as I felt after five days in the Middlesex Hospital in London, cossetted and protected.

Coming out I could not believe I'd ever deal with the traffic, the streets, the struggle of daily life. This state of mind lasted a day or two. I am sure that it would be easy to fall victim to Purdah and soon begin to think that no other way of life was possible.

The meeting with the two commanders' women went on for a long time; and for a silly reason. They were getting bored with us and wanted to get on with their lives; and we had run out of small talk and our stock of Farsi. But all the children were with us, and the men in the front room, of course, could not come through to the women's quarters: there was no child there with them to send. They sat on and on thinking we were having such a good time we didn't want to end it. At last we thought of sending a child out to them to enquire.

We made arrangements to return, to film them all with the permission of their men. This didn't happen. Other things happened but not this.

As for the woman commander Maryam, now we asked every muhjahid we met about her but they only smiled politely. They told us that the women help the muhjahidin all the time in the war; in the towns they conceal them, find them hiding places from the Russians, carry ammunition and messages, the war could not go on without the women. But a woman commander! They wouldn't hear of it. But of course she would be 'invisible', like a woman in a bhurka.

There is a tradition of women warriors in Afghanistan. For instance, there was one called Malali. She is a heroine with monuments everywhere, girls are named after her. It was at a famous battle called Maiwan, in 1882. The English General Burroughs was winning: the Afghans had been marching all night and were tired. Then Malali, a peasant girl, called the soldiers cowards, and walked out in front of them towards the British lines. She was killed, but her death energized the Afghans, and they won the battle.

It is interesting that even the women members of our party disbelieved in the existence of Maryam, smiling with the same polite disbelief as the muhjahidin, saying: 'It is enough that there is such a myth, a woman's myth.' I believed it; there was too much detail in the story for it to be a myth.

We had been trying to get into a camp that was not one of the show camps where the Pakistanis, understandably, take visitors. One even has a visitors' book for VIPS, so we were told.

The day after we failed to meet the commander whose family we visited, he turned up and took us to the same desert area to see some newly established camps. Again we drove until we had left behind the green fertile fields and the irrigation systems, and the fat contented animals, and were in a desert place, full of red blowing dust, stones, dry gulleys, rocky ridges. The good ground available for refugee camps has been used up. Poor land, or desert, or mountain areas, are all they can find now.

The party had supplied tents, some of them ragged. They were scattered about in the dust, over the ridges, a few among some sparse desert shrubs. These people came out of Afghanistan, over the mountains, six weeks ago. It has been very hot, and twenty babies and small children have died.

Some of the tents have low walls of hard mud around them, but most only a little soil roughly piled up. The tents are floored with bare earth. There is nothing in them, except for a few cooking pots. Not much food: there was a little flour in bags hanging from the corners of the tents. Flour and salt. 'Salt is cheap,' says the commander, grim. A lorry comes once a day with water: enough to drink, but not enough to wash with. There are latrine pits here and there between the tents. They are about a yard long, two feet deep. They have no covers: there is nothing to use as covers. As my mother pointed out, in another context, the sun rapidly dries the deposits, which thereafter blow about with the dust, spreading diseases. 'But ultra-violet rays kill bugs,' we hopefully assure each other.

Even in this awful place women were kept separate from the men. They and the small girls were crowded in the opening of their tents, watching the men and the boys of all ages who were everywhere, with the very small girls. A girl of about ten loses her freedom and has to join the women: before that she is as free as she will ever be in her life. When we women went towards the women's tents we were surrounded by a mass of women and children begging for medicine, any medicines. This is partly because, the poorer they are, the more ignorant, the greater their uncritical respect for Western medicine: they have never heard of the scandals that make us careful about the drugs we take. Partly they are indeed badly in need of medicines. 'And so the Russians bombed our villages and destroyed the crops standing in our fields and we came over the mountains. . .' and during the weeks of journeying, the women of all ages, and the children of all ages, with little food or water, of course fell ill, got diarrhoea, broke limbs, became rheumatic, suffered from nervous disorders, could not sleep. There were untreated wounds from the bombing. And there were no medicines, none. They

113

begged and begged, and all we had were a few aspirins which they bore off as if they were some kind of miracle.

It was horrible, moving around among these people, with nothing to give them, except the promise to publicise their situation.

Some of them were anxious to tell their stories, believing that if the world knew, help would be forthcoming. Every story began, 'The Russians bombed our village and we came over the mountains to this place.' A woman said that when the Russians find people in a village they slit up the women's stomachs, and kill the children, 'for fun'. One said that the Russians found a girl baking bread on the edge of a village when they attacked, and they threw her into her own oven and burned her to death. And laughed. Did we know the Russians piled alive people in heaps, poured petrol over them, and set them alight? Did we know that the Russians put alive people into pits, heaped earth over them, and then drove tanks back and forth over them until there wasn't any more movement? The atrocity stories go on and on. 'Do you want to hear more?' demands the commander, fiercely. We say no, thinking of our people in the West who have already supped so full of horrors not their own and who, alas, might start suffering from 'compassion fatigue'.

Some people are a long way beyond telling their stories. In one tent, where the sky is showing through rents, sits an old woman in the rags of her flight from home. The red dust of the floor of the tents has three greasy sacks on it. Her five sons have been killed fighting with the muh-jahidin. She sits there rocking, weeping, rocking, mad with grief.

It was during this visit that the commander placed a

Kalashnikov in my arms and demanded that I should be thus photographed. It happened that I had broken my wrist and it was bandaged. He would of course not ever understand why this dramatic picture might fail to delight me. I was embarrassed; he hurt that I was embarrassed. Was this not a Kalashnikov? Was I not wounded, just like one of them? I think this could fairly be described as a culture clash.

It was here, too, we saw illustrated the basic dilemma of the film photographer. Leon wanted to get pictures of this terrible suffering to show the world. There were two little boys from the extreme north of Afghanistan, orphans: they had nothing in the world. They had been found wandering on a road not far from Mazar-i-Sharif by an old Turkoman. They could not say what had happened, for they did not know. Their father and mother, brothers and sisters, had all been there with them, and then the Russian plane came over and that was all they could remember. The old Turkoman walked down with them across Afghanistan from North to South, which took many days, begging for their food and for his; he came out of Afghanistan across the mountains with them and brought them to this camp, this place of refuge, this scattering of ragged tents in a desert place with little food or water. He found a family that would take them in. They were still in shock. Their faces were stunned and empty. Leon wanted to question them while he filmed them and a muhjahid knelt by them, trying to make them repeat their story. They could not, and began to cry. Leon was upset, the bystanders were upset, it was all awful.

And the refugees are still streaming in and in. Now many thousands, hundreds of thousands are dying when they arrive. The Pakistanis are not registering any more refugees, they cannot cope, and who can blame them? The International Relief Agencies help, but do not help enough. Four million people are a lot of people. Western countries take in a few thousand refugees here and there and make great claims for themselves. The Pakistanis have taken in millions and have been doing so for seven years, and they are not a rich nation.

I have not mentioned the half million to a million (I have just heard, two million) refugees, in Iran. If the refugees in Pakistan are in a bad way, then those in Iran are much worse. Recently a limited access was given to the Red Cross to inspect some of the camps. Iran has just made a pact with the Soviet Union, and what is going to happen to the refugees? Even before the pact Khomeini was handing over the muhjahidin coming out of the fighting to visit their families, straight into the hands of the Russians. Somebody, being told of this, asked an Afghan, 'But how does he reconcile this with his being a Moslem?' He replied grimly that it pleased him to have the basics stated, innocently, like this.

All this time we were still trying to set up meetings with educated or professional women Afghan refugees. Discussing this beforehand we had agreed that we wanted to hear such a woman state, in so many words, that in spite of suffering in Pakistan from all the disadvantages of Purdah, of being veiled, she nevertheless was protesting against the invasion of her country by the Russians, who were claiming to have freed women. But soon we became embarrassed at this formulation, realizing that we had been affected by Russian propaganda without even knowing it. It would be impossible to find an Afghan refugee woman

116

who would need to say this: it would go without saying.

A woman called, let us say, Amina, was described to us as typical of a whole range or type of Afghan woman. Educated, or part educated, and free in Afghanistan to wear western dress, and to go unveiled, she got herself additional education or training , perhaps as a nurse, or an accountant. Her family, including her father, supported her in her efforts. She married an engineer, highly qualified; and this was a good marriage, for her husband wanted an educated and emancipated wife. Then came The Catastrophe, and she ran away from the Russians across the mountains with her small children, pregnant with another, who died soon after being born. She is in one of the better refugee camps, with two tiny rooms and a little verandah. Suddenly she is surrounded by women with traditional ideas, with whom in Afghanistan she would have had no contact. They recognize her as better educated than themselves and with all kinds of dangerous modern notions which she cannot conceal. The enviousness of the worse off, exacerbated by hard times and by the mullahs who roam the camps to search out wrong-doing, laying down the Law, persecutes this woman. She is back in Purdah, and she has to cover her face if she leaves the woman's room, which is the back room. The slightest infringement of Purdah is reported to the mullahs. She is in a party camp, dependent on them for food, and her children will suffer for her misdemeanours. She is in what amounts to imprisonment, with no way out until the end of the war in Afghanistan.

'If you do not manage to interview such a woman, and you will certainly find it hard to film her, then you can write this story. It is the story of a very large number of women,' says the Afghan man who told it to us.

Attempts to interview and film educated Afghan women continued, and always mysteriously failed.

A woman who worked in a school said there would be 'no problem' if we went to her place to film her. But this phrase 'no problem' always signifies something going wrong, in my experience. In order to avoid the thousand spying eyes of those busy alleyways, we suggested that she should come to us in the hotel: no one need ever know. She came one evening as the light was going, heavily veiled of course and accompanied by a male member of her family, as was correct. We went to my room in the hotel. There, as usual, as wrappers came off this parcel of a woman, she was revealed as a lively, bright creature – just like you or I. Would she like to eat in my room where she would be unobserved, we asked? Or perhaps, we suggested daringly, on the lawn? By then it was completely dark. To sit out in a garden after being imprisoned in those stuffy rooms night after night. . .she said yes. She could not resist it. Her brother said yes, he said he thought it would be all right: who would see her? So we sat around, several of us, on the dark lawn; and we listened to her laments, and her brother's, for the lost freedoms of Kabul before The Catastrophe. And then an unlucky thing happened. A man from her little net of streets suddenly appeared at our table: he wanted to be invited to sit down and join us, he wanted to work as a film technician. A day or two before he had followed us around as we went about the quarter. He had pursued us. We had not been able to get rid of him: we did not like him. Suddenly he saw our guest, the unveiled Afghan girl, and then looked again closely. She sat trembling. This being Peshawar, Paranoid City, we were all thinking that he had been sent by the area Eye, the little

118

policeman, to check on this poor girl, having heard somehow that she had left her room for that one evening. For
after all she did stay in it every night. Could it really be just
chance? The man hung about, he would not go, and the
girl sat there, frozen. 'Is this going to be bad for you?' we
whispered. 'Oh, no problem, no problem,' she said. When
at last he went she asked to be taken to the loo, where I
believe she was sick.

The liberal Mullah who, when interviewed, said, 'Is it
Islam or is it men that oppress women?' would certainly
not approve of this scene. But it was going on far below
him in the hierarchy. Probably from his point of view the
little bully of a policeman was an unimportant person. I am
sure the Mullah would scarcely know of this level of petty
bullying and persecution. Why am I sure? Because, my
masters, it is easy to observe this process going on everywhere in every country in the world. 'What? Are you
telling me *my* policemen take bribes, beat up innocents,
fake evidence? Of course not!' 'Are you saying that the
officials of *my* department are corrupt down there at the
lower levels? What nonsense!'

A new plan evolved: this girl and her mother and her
father would come to us on their Sunday, which is a Friday
and they could all tell us, and the cameras, of their experi-
ences. Then we would have lunch, *inside* the hotel room
where it would be safe. Afterwards, the women veiled,
we would go to a museum. This would be a big treat for
the women and remind them of life in a sensible country,
they said. But that morning a young man appeared, a
messenger from the family. Alas, alas, the mother was sick
and of course her daughter had to stay and nurse her.

Some days later the policeman remembered the promise

he had made to allow us to film and interview educated women, and he arrived at the hotel with two bundled-up girls. They were trainee nurses. He simply would not go away, which meant that they could not unveil, and that meant that they could not be filmed. He was at last persuaded to depart, and went, in a very bad temper. The girls flung off their veils and became chatty, friendly, ordinary girls, thrilled at this chance of getting out of the restrictions of their lives. At the end of precisely fifteen minutes he came back. So they had to re-veil and he took them off home.

The leitmotif, the theme of our visit, which might be called 'The Vanishing Ladies' continued to impose itself. Sitting around – (and sitting around) – we planned and plotted how to outwit these poor women's jailers. But we failed. And of course there was always another possible reason: those with relatives still in Afghanistan are afraid to emerge from their shadows. Using relatives as hostages or levers is a favourite Russian technique.

Nancy and I decided to fly up to Chitral in the Himalayas, a half-hour's flight. It was a little plane, with the usual meltingly beautiful air hostess. By now I had understood why the few women in public places are all beautiful. Having banished women's faces indoors, so that all one sees out of doors are men, men, crowds of melancholy men, when they do have an excuse for a woman's face to be visible, the Pakistanis naturally make sure it is a pretty face. I suppose this could be described as hypocrisy.

We dodged in and out of mountains. Beneath us were the endless intricacies of terracing all over the hills and mountainsides. They were like green fish scales, or like sequins. At Chitral airport we were met by a man from the

Mountain View Inn in a jeep: no ordinary car can cope with Chitral's roads. We were told we had to report immediately to the police HQ, like everyone else. Chitral is an area of military significance with the Russians only a few miles away over one range of mountains in Afghanistan, and the Chinese over another. Afghanistan's jagged and snow-covered peaks were just there at the end of the road.

In the Police Station we hung about and about, and I was fascinated by the great wooden board that had on it the lists of all the District Officers, starting from the end of the last century. Until 1947, the date of the liberation of the Indian sub-continent from the British, the names were all English, very English, the 'Turtons and Burtons' of the British Empire. I noticed they were stationed up here for only a year. I imagined a young man posted to Chitral's mountainous solitudes to represent The Empire. Easy to picture him, for I have known so many of them; stiff, shy, stubbornly convinced of the worth of the Empire, on the whole honest. He was conscientious, and without a rupee's worth of insight into the people who surrounded him. I was not least intrigued that while I was absorbed by the tale told by the great board, of young men posted up here among hostile tribes, Nancy was not at all interested. For me it was a tale of people who might have known my parents and grandparents. For her the British Empire was somebody else's history.

We were at last told to present ourselves to the Chief of Police. He was a heavily built, decent-looking man, in uniform of course, behind a desk loaded with papers. As lower ranks came in with messages or chits, they saluted, heels together, then relaxed at once and stood very much at ease – evidently his subordinates did not find this man intimidating.

He kept us talking and talking.

Anywhere in the West two women of indeterminate age wandering about with cameras are as 'invisible' as a woman in a bhurka in an Islamic country. Who would take a second look? Here we were a challenge, or an offence, to every eye, and puzzled this policeman. There was Nancy, covered all over with cameras and equipment; and we were telling the truth, which was that we wanted to go and see a doctor Nancy knew, who runs a clinic for Afghans called Freedom Medicine. 'Of course,' said we, 'the authorities must know of this doctor.' Oh no said the official, who could we possibly mean? This absurdity went on for quite a time. He wanted to know if the object of our journey was to visit Khafir Kalash, which is the great tourist attraction of these parts; a medieval tribe. All the books I have read about this area describe something like Merrie England as it actually must have been. A lot of song and dance certainly, very picturesque, but filthy, smelly and generally unappetising. Yes, yes, we said, we did want to see the Khafir Kalash tribe but not on this visit; perhaps on another visit. We were abashed by the differences of perspective thus displayed, for we belong to that minority of the world's population who can say, 'Oh yes, do let's go back to Pakistan, it's so beautiful and we didn't see— '.

Chat continued. We asked if there was skiing in the winter, having been told that there was. He said that Chitral in winter was awful and he seemed ground into gloom at the thought of it. I asked if he would be more pleased to see us in the winter, and he did smile. Then we were taken off to another office where we were issued with passes for two days.

There are places so beautiful they freeze your senses. Chitral is one. It is built low between mountains that tower and loom. In some places white peaks mingle with white clouds. Pretty mountain streams dash about everywhere. Even in September the sun does not present itself before about eight in the morning and departs at four-thirty: what can this place be like in winter? Long long hours of night, hours of gloomy half-daylight with short sad moments when the sun can reach down to lay warm fingers on the little town. We could see why the Police Chief dreaded the winter. Back in the hotel the extent of gardens revealed themselves. They are large and have all the same plants and shrubs as would be in a hotel garden in Zimbabwe. This hotel, however, was absolutely unlike the country hotels of, let's say, the mountains in the Vumba, which are all drinking hotels. The Mountain View Inn was put up in the sixties, a relaxed, graceful, two-storied building, with wide verandahs. In Peshawar I would not have believed that I could come to see Dean's Hotel as civilization itself, but the Mountain View Inn's pretensions are indicated by this exchange: 'Can we have some soda water please, with lemon?'

Manager: 'We don't have soda water, this isn't Peshawar, you know.'

There was Coca-Cola, 7-Up, and then more Coca-Cola.

We had to hire a jeep and of course the driver was a member of the police, an amiable and helpful fellow, aided by a Nuristani who looked quite classically English. He kept telling me in broken English how much he liked the English.

We drove off in the jeep to see if the American doctor was there. The hospital is in the process of construction, but the by now familiar tents with mud walls around them, full of busy trainee muhjahidin, had been put up in the courtyard. As we two approached the doctor called, 'And do I hear the English language – again!' As this place is so close to the Afghan border journalists arrive by day and by night. They are entertained, shown everything, and then they go off, 'And then,' enquires the doctor, 'what happens to those articles? If they are written, they are not printed.' Then follows the conversation that we seem to be having several times a day, about why the western press printed the Russian point of view but not the Afghan one.

This man and his wife run a large centre to train Afghan fighters as medical aides, to go in with the muhjahidin into battle. That place is somewhere not far from Peshawar, but this one is the nearest clinic to the actual fighting, the doctor explains. 'Also, this is the road that most refugees use coming out of Afghanistan. It is the only place that women and children from the local camps can come for medical treatment. Today there would normally be queues waiting for the female doctor who flies up here two or three times a week from Peshawar but they have kept away because they have heard somehow she is not here today.' They wouldn't go to a man doctor, no matter how ill. He said that tomorrow we could come and film. Of course we could film the women! (No problem!) Off we went, back to the hotel. There a communal meal had been set out on the verandah. It was a dim scene. For some reason I still haven't sorted out, two evenings a week the hotel's lights don't work, and there are candles. At supper there was a Swedish freelance photographer, a Dutch woman working in a hospital for Afghan women and children in Peshawar and her husband, in some sort of construction work up here in Chitral. They had their small

124

child with them. The meal over, there was nothing to do but go to bed. Neither Nancy or I ever go to bed before one or two, but here we obediently tucked ourselves up by ten o'clock. On the verandah various Pakistanis, male, sat chatting with the hotel owner, a plump young man of – it goes without saying – great charm. I am sure that during the long winter this hotel, which does not close, is the centre of local (male) society. Still sleepless, I lay awake and listened to Chitral's night sounds. A litter of puppies somewhere close were wakeful and yapped frantically off and on all night. A donkey brayed out the sorrows of the universe. The men went to their rooms along the verandah, still amiably gossiping. Water was running noisily nearby and mosquitoes hummed along the walls. Soon the cock crowed. Then the Call to Prayer at ten to five. Chitral is not a large town. It has a pretty mosque with a good-sized minaret: you'd think that one Call would be enough. But for a few minutes half a dozen sonorous male voices called the town to stumble out of bed and pray. I dressed in the dark, clumsily, because of my broken wrist, and looked out. Already some bearded and turbaned men were at their prayers on the still dim lawns. They stood, then prostrated themselves; knelt, and prostrated themselves. An energetic business, prayer in Islam. Did the originator of these exercises think: 'If the prayers have to be accompanied by certain prescribed movements, and the movements are designed to exercise the whole body, they'll all be kept healthy?' Five times a day, strict Moslems (male) go through what amounts to a work-out.

By the time they had finished, the tops of the mountains were glowing with light.

The bathroom had the most original shower I've seen.

The bathroom is simply a very large cement room. It has in it a wardrobe of Victorian dimensions. Was a Victorian wardrobe washed up here from the wreck of the Raj? There was a basin with all manner of electric sockets for razors, shaving lights and so forth – the last word in modern equipment. There was a lavatory on a little pedestal. The shower stuck out of a wall in the corner and floods the entire floor when used. Why not? The floor was thus washed clean at the same time as the person using it.

We breakfasted at six a.m. in a dining room that could easily feed two hundred. What occasion would fill it? Two long tables, covered by the filthiest tablecloths I have ever seen stood at right angles, occupying most of the space; but there was a small solitary table and at this we breakfasted in the company of a sorrowing widower, who told us that, his wife being dead and he being lonely, he spends his time travelling the world. He had been fortunate in his choice of Pakistan, so full of beauty spots, as a holiday place. He was the most villainous-looking man. One temple was a crater from some old wound. An arms dealer? Drugs? Just a plain little old ordinary spy? Perhaps even an old-fashioned one, dedicated to the interests of one country? He was, I think, German or Dutch.

Chitral was one of the trading posts of the old Silk Road. The word 'silk' feeds a tinge of glamour or luxury into the image; but the road was never more than a stony track, here running along the sides of mountains with a plunge down to the river beneath. The caravan beasts must have been strung out one at a time. In the Chitral bazaar, the main street, you go back several hundred years. It is a rough, steep lane, lined with the usual booths of mud, or mud and straw, the roofs piled with mud. They sell everything as they always have, but now some of the goods are plastic. The whole place is crammed with the muhjahidin wandering about, buying food for their families in the refugee camps, drinking tea in the minute tea houses. We looked for things to buy and then went off in the jeep to the doctor's clinic. But the woman doctor had not come from Peshawar and so there were no queues of women to film or to photograph. We decided to take the jeep up the road to Garam Chasma, which means 'warm springs'. This takes two hours, not because of the distance but because of the roads which are terrible. Sometimes we stopped to give some muhjahid a lift. It was stunningly, awe-fully beautiful. The road runs anywhere it can fit itself along the mountains. Sometimes the river has in it boulders the size of houses.

After about half an hour's drive there were a lot of white tents with the walls, all over a hillside. This was a muhjahidin camp. There were hundreds of men on that hill. We stopped and the driver came too, to look after us. But there was no need to be worried. The week after I came home I saw a film of the muhjahidin which makes them look like crazed, drug-ridden savages. If a film were shown on TV of this camp, the impression would be of friendly well-mannered men in a well ordered camp. From their point of view it must have been hard to be suddenly faced with two unveiled infidel women and, in any case, this camp being on the main road, journalists appear far too often. They behaved with impeccable courtesy. In one tent they were sleeping, in another they sat around talking. One wrote a letter home to his family, others were reading books and newspapers, one in English. A muhjahid sat out in the space between the tents cooking a meal of vegetables fried in dough with some kind of sauce: it certainly was not going to be a lavish meal. As we left the tents there was laughter and joking – at our expense. They were copying our 'Tashakur' 'Tashakur' ('Thank you' 'Thank you') in high female voices. This could have been raucous or hostile but it was quite good-natured.

We drove on up the pass. At Garam Chasma the driver put us in a little orchard and brought us green tea from the Chaikhana. Just beyond the orchard men were high on the brick wall of a new building, they were working with a lot of laughter and jokes. The wall looked flimsy, but anything human would seem slight and unimportant among these mountains. There were hundreds of horses in green meadows. They all looked fat: it was the end of summer. During the hours we were there the horses were being taken in groups down to the river to drink by the muhjahidin.

We were lucky, arriving as muhjahidin were preparing to go off into the mountains to fight. Destination: Panjshir. It would take them some days to get there. They walk almost continuously, stopping four hours in the twenty-four, when they eat bread, drink green tea and sleep a little. They go in with supplies of their bread, the thick flat *nan* of the region. When they at last reach their hideouts their feet are swollen to the knees and they have to rest. All they wear is sandals. When the snows come many lose their toes, or even feet.

Late afternoon. September sunlight lit the green meadow high above the village where the men, hundreds of them, went about their business of loading their glossy horses. They had their blankets slung over their shoulders with their beloved Kalashnikovs. While this was going on,

I was sitting in the jeep by myself in the main street of the village, just opposite the little tea house crowded with muhjahidin taking a last meal before journey. They kept passing and passing the jeep, in ones, or twos, or groups, and they stopped. A white female in a jeep? I must be a doctor. They asked for medicine over and over again. They were going in to fight without medicines, without a doctor. I had to say no, no, I was sorry, I had none. They asked simply and directly, and took the refusal like those used to being stoically disappointed. This 'street' was really a lane of hard, rutted mud between mud and straw buildings. Again, this could have been hundreds of years ago, except for the weapons the men were carrying.

Donkeys came past too, strings of them, little donkeys stepping nimbly among the ruts and the stones. They were well fed, but they had sores, all of them, from badly fitting girths and straps. By the end of this winter the donkeys would not be looking like this, and all these fat horses – well, many of them – would be dead. There is not enough food.

The lines of men with their horses went off up the pass and disappeared into the mountains.

We went back to Chitral. If Chitral had made Peshawar seem like a metropolis, then now Chitral, beside Garam Chashma, was civilisation itself. But we were thinking of the fighters moving up into the mountains in the night. It would be very dark, there was no moon. It would be silent too: perhaps only the sound of hooves on stones and the night birds. We had been told, had read, of careless, noisy muhjahidin attracting the attention of the enemy, but this lot had seemed sober and alert and responsible.

We went back in the jeep to Freedom Medicine for

129

supper, as invited, and found a crisis. On the verandah of the half-finished hospital the group of muhjahidin being trained as medical aides were sitting with Doctor Brenner. An administrative muddle was closing this clinic: they hoped not permanently. There is no other clinic at all in these parts, either for muhjahidin, or for the thousands upon thousands in the near refugee camps. The building would have to be left empty; they would take down the tents. Some would now have to devote themselves to the long manouvring with petty bureaucracy, which takes up so much of everyone's time here and which puts this characteristic look of patient determination on their faces. Just like the expressions of the muhjahidin when I said I had no medicines for them.

Doctor Brenner said it was always a question of sticking it out. When he started his first clinic he had no money at all. He appealed for money after he had begun building. It came. It always came, but it was never enough. When things seemed hopeless, money came in from somewhere. He talked as I have heard religious people talk: 'God will provide'. Before we left this group, sitting patiently on their little verandah, the still unfinished operating room behind them – sitting together perhaps for the last time, if the bureaucratic decision went against them, – we asked if any of them had heard of the woman commander of Herat, who had men fighting under her. Small, polite smiles, which said that such a thing was impossible.

Again we went to bed soon after the last Call to Prayer. The group of men on the verandah talked quietly, sleepily. It really did seem as if all Chitral was asleep, but perhaps – we hoped – inside the houses there was fun going on, conversations, perhaps between men and women. There might even be a party or two. But they were all supposed to get up at five; and they did get up at five, so this was probably their bedtime. I thought of the Chief of Police's complaint about the dreary winters: did that mean that autumn evenings in Chitral were feasts of pleasure?

Perhaps next time we visited Chitral everything would be different. The enterprising manager is building a tea room, for there is no tea room in Chitral for Western visitors. It will look over roofs and gardens, and across the river to the mountains, which seem to say so loudly, 'This too will pass'. Down through this valley came the armies of Alexander the Great, and the Mongols. Now the Russians are just behind that range there, biding their time.

The manager says, 'Perhaps next summer the Americans will come back and then we'll all get rich', and he laughs. He shares European affectionate impatience with the Americans for letting themselves be bothered by a few bombs. He, like everyone, says, 'But why, when people are killing each other in their cities all the time?' He shrugs. As do we all.

The jeep driver, that is, the agent of the police in charge of us, had told us that we should film the mosque and to be sure to get there at first light, which of course, in this pit between the mountains, would be late. When we set off to get to the mosque and asked the way, several turbaned grey-beards pretended not to understand the word 'mosque', which was visible: we didn't know which path to take. Back to the hotel we went and were told it was this road, and not that, and to take no notice of the mullahs. We walked in crowds of children in uniforms going to school: the modern world. The mosque is pretty, light, airy, graceful, its cupolas tinted different colours. It seemed to float there in the first sunlight. From a distance it is a vision of what a mosque should be; but it has been badly built and is already stained and cracked. A couple of the mad mullahs jealously kept an eye on Nancy while she took pictures of their mosque.

Then we went back into the stream of schoolchildren. Behind us came a regiment of soldiers. They were making for another old dilapidated building which was probably the palace in which former rulers took their pleasure. It had wonderful tiles over the entrance: we wanted to look at them but were hesitating about going there if it was Army property. Nancy dropped a bit of equipment from a camera. The officer in charge picked it up on the point of a bayonet, handed it to her with a bow, and invited us in with a smile. We followed the soldiers into a big empty court surrounded by rooms that are falling down, into which the soldiers quickly vanished. What for, we wondered? What could soldiers be doing in these ruins? It was melancholy there in the old palace, which would soon be yet another mound of earth saying that a building had once stood there.

We were booked on the second flight out of Chitral that morning. This is a simple statement of something achieved with difficulty and much queueing.

The airline offices in Chitral are a dingy little room whose verandah, a few feet square, has a ticket window overlooking it and a rushing stream that appears from one wall and disappears under another. To get inside the room you need to be nimble, stepping from bank to bank. Frustrated crowds press against that window whenever the office is open. We women, spied in the mass of men, were at once called inside, where we could not be seen by them. They gave us tickets on that over-full plane. They are always over-full. To fly out of Chitral is a tricky bit of navigation between the mountains, and at the slightest hint of bad weather there are no flights at all. There is always a backlog of hopeful passengers crowding around that window. We were desperate to get out of Chitral. Suppose the bad weather closed in while we were there? Why we might have to spend the winter there! The only other way in, but not in winter, is the ten-hour road journey, picturesque, but so appalling that people who have made it say, 'Well, it is certainly something you should do – once'. Provisions to last a whole winter have to be brought up in autumn. The road is closed with the first snows, and the aircraft may or may not fly.

When we goat-footed our way out of that office across the little mountain stream, a muhjahid asked, 'How did you get into the office when we can't?'

'Ah, but you see,' Nancy replied with simple dignity, 'we are women.'

At the airport we said goodbye to the jeep driver and his urchin Nuristani assistant with genuine sadness. 'You are a marvellous driver' I said sincerely, thinking of how he had eased that jeep for hours and hours over the awful road. At this moment the jeep began to run backwards – he had forgotten to put the brake on. People leapt laughing out of the way, the jeep was secured and we were delivered into the airport building. Then a man in the ordinary Pakistani dress that looks like pyjamas, asked to see our passports. Nancy suddenly became a true daughter of the American Revolution and said haughtily that she was not in the habit of showing her passport to just anybody who asked. To back her up I said he wasn't wearing any identity disc. The poor fellow was astounded: he was, of course, from the Police Station, making sure that we were actually leaving. He fumbled in a pocket and brought out a photograph on a document that said he was 'Security'. It was folded in a bit of old paper. At this we handed over our passports. We were sad to leave Chitral.

There, because it is the end of the earth, a little mountain airport, extremes meet; no buffet but a man brings you individual orders of tea on a tray where you sit. Then Nancy and I were banished into Purdah through Immigration. They made Nancy take every bit of her camera equipment apart, naturally enough. As for me, I had to take off the Velcro'd cast on my broken wrist in case drugs, or perhaps even a bomb, were hidden underneath it. They are (of course) dazzlingly pretty girls who do this work. They were laughing, embarrassed but determined, as they prodded various bits of my anatomy. Purdah in Chitral airport is a little room for women and small children. It was full. In Purdah women gaze out of windows and keep opening doors quickly a little way to see what might be happening on the other side; it is a place where you listen and watch for the big events going on outside the room you are imprisoned in.

There was not a seat empty on the plane. They escorted off a young man, tall, long haired, vintage sixties, American, who was stoned and silly, and then they brought him back on the plane again. A security man with a gun rode in front with the pilot all the way. We wondered if there had been another bomb, or airport incident that we had not read about: we had not been reading any newspapers in Chitral.

We descended into the dust haze of Peshawar. In

Dean's Hotel the fans revolved in the thick air. My time was running out. Just before I left I met, not the educated woman that we had been trying to find, but a certain male professor. It was a man who put most eloquently the case for his female compatriots. He was Professor Majruh, who was Professor of Literature in Kabul and now works in Peshawar University. He says 'I hear you've been meeting the muhjahidin. Great characters, yes, I know. But I tell you, I would a thousand times rather be a muhjahid than one of their women. A muhjahid has to suffer great hardship, he may have to live for months on very little food, he has no warm clothes, when they get wounded they usually die for lack of medical attention, many of them get killed. But all that is better than being an Afghan woman in one of these terrible camps. We are mountain people and desert people, we are used to space, no one is cramped for space in Afghanistan, in the towns or out of them. The women had a good life before The Catastrophe, very few were veiled, women were not forced to be veiled, the power of the mullahs was nothing compared to what it is now. It is a tragedy of this war that the mullahs have achieved so much influence. The Afghans are not a fanatical people by nature, though when you hear them talk about the Jihad, you may think they are. It is this war that has intensified what was only an aspect of their character.

'The women have all stopped singing', says the Professor, memorably, 'Once, before The Catastrophe, what you heard in the villages was women singing. Now they are cooped up like animals in their camps, with no end in sight to their war, with their children. Their men are fighting, they come and visit them between battles, sometimes with months between visits. The women are depressed, as I

135

read your women are sometimes, and live on sedatives, when they are lucky enough to get any. They are forced to go into Purdah and wear the veil, they cannot leave the camps, they are policed by the mullahs and by the Pakistan camp authorities. No, I am not criticising the Pakistanis, without them we would all be dead, there would be no Afghans left.'

Then he talked about the killing of the Afghan intellectuals by the Russians. A whole generation of poets, playwrights, writers, intellectuals have vanished into their prisons and they have not been heard of since. There was a literary movement developing in Afghanistan, something quite new and very promising. All these people have simply been wiped out. Why has the world not protested? Has this ever happened before in our time, that a whole generation of intellectuals has simply been destroyed with not one word of protest from anyone? The list of their names would fill that wall there from top to bottom, all tortured and murdered and not a whisper of protest.'

At last we found a woman we could interview and film without supervision by some self-appointed monitor. What had previously seemed so hard to do became simple as these things do when they happen after long difficulties. It is hard to imagine that anyone could make Tajwar Kakar do anything she did not want to do. She is a small woman but vigorous, decisive, full of confidence. She lives in the usual poor conditions with her seven children, five girls and two boys, whom she supports as a teacher. She works very hard.

She was in Kunduz in northern Afghanistan and became involved in the Resistance immediately after the Communist coup in 1978. With the aid of male Resistance commanders she established a school to train boys in arms and explosives. She instigated or took part in many demonstrations against the Communist regime, and when the Russians invaded in 1980 she was given the task of carrying money, food and clothes to the families of men in Kabul who were in prison or dead. There she got a job as a teacher and was involved actively in the underground.

She was threatened with arrest by Communist Party members. She said, 'You people are hypocrites, your words are beautiful but your actions are ugly.' She was arrested and tortured. She did not give the Russians any information. She was put in solitary because she was 'such a bad example to the other women prisoners.' They got nothing out of her. She was released and went back to Kunduz. There she continued in the Resistance until a man who knew all about her was appointed as KHAD officer in Kunduz. She fled with her family to Kabul with the aid of the muhjahidin. When we asked her our routine question, 'The Russians say they are bringing freedom to the women of Afghanistan, and what do you have to say to that?', she laughed and said that before The Catastrophe no women were ever in prison, now the prisons in Afghanistan are full of women.

It emerged quite casually that there are women in the Resistance. 'In Herat there is a lady Resistance fighter whose father was a freedom fighter and was killed. Then her brother replaced him as commander and was killed. She took her brother's place and formed an independent group of women fighters. They were given arms by the muhjahidin and carry out operations on their own account.'

And the woman called Maryam with three thousand

men under her? By now this interest of ours which had been in the forefront when we first came to Peshawar had lost its importance, had come to seem frivolous, even typical western sensationalism, or gimmickry. What did it matter who was fighting? It certainly wouldn't matter to them. For them it is the fight that counts.

I flew back via Islamabad on my way home. If I had had as bad a seat flying to Peshawar as I had flying back, I would never have known about that landscape which is like a battleground between Man and Nature.

I was in a hotel for the night. The theme of sleeplessness continues: I stood by the window from one a.m. onwards, listening and watching. It was hot and muggy, it smelled of dust, petrol, spices, sewage. The sounds, so different from London, kept my ears on the alert. In Islamabad too, people go to bed early; but there was a light on in an upper storey and from this flowed all night the sound of singing. A man was singing, sad, slow, all longing and deprivation. Just below me among the parked cars the hotel watchman sat through the night accompanied by some cronies, three or four of them. These men, turbaned, bearded, grave, drank tea, went off, wandered back, their low voices a continuous murmur unless a bus or a private car, making an early start to beat the heat and the traffic, set off for somewhere. The light in the upper window did not go out, and the song went on and on. Then came the Call to Prayer, which sounded melancholy and yearning, like the man's song. It was a sad duet.

Each day I am away from Pakistan I find myself admiring it more. In Peshawar people are cynical about Pakistan's motives, they say that aid and arms for the refugees get stolen, that the authorities can be bribed, that the very existence of the refugee camps has boosted the economy. All that may be true, but I came back from Pakistan to news of workers, once accepted into Europe, because it suited us, being sent back home. Not only in Europe: Arabia is sending back foreign workers. We met some in Peshawar. What a song and dance we make about the few refugees we do take in, the rich countries of Europe. But General Zia has remained imperturbable: he will not return the refugees to the Russians.

Benazir Bhutto, on the other hand, has said that if she gets into power she will send them home.

November 1986

Some 'Stingers' – the ground-to-air missiles – are now reaching the muhjahidin. Not as many as has been claimed; not enough to enable them to win, but the fact that there are any at all must be doing everything for their morale.

December 1986

As this book goes to press, the news is that the Russians are offering six months' cease-fire on certain conditions. They, of course, know that these conditions will not be accepted by the muhjahidin, whose agreement must be obtained if the fighting is to end.

What are the Russians trying to achieve? What effects can already be seen?

139

1. Just as when the Russians announced the withdrawal of a small number of troops in the autumn, people are saying, 'Oh well, it is all right, the war is ending, isn't it?' with a relieved look, and the unspoken corollary that they needn't bother about it, there is no need to think about it. This aspect of the new offer repeats Russian propaganda since the start of the war, all aimed to lessen western involvement in, concern about, the war.

2. Pakistan is even more divided than it was about the Afghan refugees: Pakistan – if not Zia's government, then another – may decide to return the refugees. Whether they are returned or not, an unstable country is even more unstabilized.

3. Some of the muhjahidin will be tempted to give in. Some may give in, though I think not many. But the effect must be to weaken and confuse the Resistance. On the other hand, this very confusion, a sharp new element in the war, may intensify the Resistance, or shake it into new patterns.

Of course the Russians want to end the war. But they want to end it on their terms. I think this offer may have explosive results, far beyond what the Russians envisage now. For instance, if Pakistan crumbles into chaos, then they will certainly be tempted to invade – with what consequences? Or, a developing situation (in all kinds of directions not foreseen by the Russians) may force on them much more international intervention than they want. Certainly, if the muhjahidin and the refugees are forcibly sent home, only the most stringent international monitoring will prevent mass murder. The more international intervention, the more likelihood of a type of government that the Russians certainly do not want.

Is it possible that this offer comes into the category of Russian behaviour described by the military man on page 59: because of their inflexibility, if something is going badly they don't try a different tactic, but intensify the methods they are already using, and sometimes destroy what they are trying to save.

If on the other hand by the time this book comes out in March there is a real acknowledgement of the muhjahidin demands, then the Russian leopard will be seen to have changed its spots.

Meanwhile, the Afghans, both inside and outside Afghanistan, badly need help.

I have just heard that the clinic run by Freedom Medicine in Chitral has been given permission by the Pakistan government to continue its work. Money can be sent to:

> Freedom Medicine
> 941 River Street
> Suite 201
> Honolulu, Hawaii 96817

> The Afghan Relief Fund
> P.O. Box 176
> Los Altos
> California 94021

Also to:

> Afghan Relief
> Registered Charity No. 289910
> PO Box 457
> London NW2 4BR

or by Direct Bank Transfer
        Messrs C. Hoare & Co.
        16 Waterloo Place
        London SW1Y 4BH
        Acc. Afghan Relief no. 93322000.

January 1987

PART THREE

*Interviews With
Mrs Tajwar Kakar*

Afghan Information Centre
Monthly Bulletin
No 57, December 1985

Tajwar Sultan, A Resistance Fighter

Mrs Tajwar Kakar, known in the resistance as Tajwar Sultan, is thirty-seven years old and is the mother of seven children (five girls and two boys). With her family she is now living as a refugee in Peshawar (Pakistan).

She was promoted from the Teachers' Training College and served as a teacher and school headmaster in Kunduz city in northern Afghanistan. She became actively involved in the resistance soon after the Communist coup of April 1978. She established, with the male Resistance commanders of the province, a school in the small village of Choqor Qishlaq which trained boys in the use of arms and explosives. She was admitted to a meeting of Jamiat (Prof. Rabani) Resistance commanders in which some well-known figures such as Oazi Islamuddin, Nek Mohammad Khan, Maulawi Adbul Samad were present. Her proposal to the meeting was:

1. No freedom fighter, especially the commanders, should marry until the end of the war.

2. Resistance fighters released from prison ten or twenty days after their arrest by the Communist authorities should not be trusted.

145

3. In order to prevent enemy infiltration in the ranks of the resistance, a special organization to investigate the background of every fighter should be clearly established.

On the occasion of the first anniversary of the Communist regime in April 1979, Tajwar and her colleagues decided to disrupt the official observance ceremony. The teachers were ordered to bring the school children to the parade ground. Tajwar and her lady friends provided some children with rubber balloons and toy explosives. When the parade started, here and there the balloons started bursting and the small explosives exploding. Some women in the crowd shouted: 'Muhjahidin are coming!' People started running. Some simple soldiers on guard around the parade ground fired their guns. It was panic. The parading party members ran for cover. The official tribune was in confusion. Many people were hurt in the rush. Even the wife of the provincial governor was injured and admitted to a hospital. The ceremony was cancelled.

Then the authorities decided to celebrate the first of May, 'Workers Day'. The ladies did not want to remain passive spectators. A day prior to the festivity, they told some of their good pupils to capture wasps and keep them alive in small boxes. There was again a huge crowd. Armed party activists, shouting slogans and carrying banners, flags and large portraits of the regime leaders started marching in a military order. The crowd pushed by underground Resistance members came closer and closer. The children, as if out of control, were running in between the marching ranks and were opening their boxes under the feet of the paraders. The wasps went inside trousers and skirts and started stinging. The paraders stopped shouting slogans. They were running in circles, throwing away

146

everything they had on them. But the children had over-done their job. There were too many wasps. People in the crowd were stung. They were shrieking and running. It was a mess. The ceremony could not be resumed. Tajwar said: '*That day hundreds of the leaders' portraits, shirts, etc. were lying on the ground. And in the confusion we collected twenty-five light arms and pistols. The machine guns were sent to the muhjahidin in the countryside and the pistols were handed over to the women working in the military section of the urban underground resistance.*'

Disguised as a village woman entirely veiled and under the pretext of a personal petition, she would go from one administrative office to another in order to find the Resistance connections, and exchange information. She held a meeting of Resistance fighters in her own house. There were eighteen men and she was elected as the person in charge of women Resistance groups. The muhjahidin from Panjsher strongly supported her nomination.

Then a committee to help families of Resistance prisoners and martyrs was created. Money, food and clothes were collected and she was given the task of going to Kabul to distribute them among the needy families of the capital. That is how she came to Kabul. It was the beginning of 1980 and the Russians had invaded the country. She found a job as a teacher in Ghafoor Nadim School. She said there were 7,000 pupils (boys and girls) in the school, 300 teachers, 200 of them women. The head of the school was a Khalqi party member and only twenty women teachers were members of the party. The rest were against the regime and many among them were actively working with the Resistance. All of them, however, were ready to take part in the demonstrations, disseminate night letters or do other risky jobs.

In Kabul she became active in the organizational work of the underground Resistance movement. She took part in the preparation of the popular uprising against the Russians in March 1980. Well connected with male Resistance groups, the women organized themselves in three sections: 1. Investigation of people collaborating with the enemy. 2. Pursuit of suspects and discovering their connections. 3. Operational group. The most active in an operation group against the enemy was a girl called Fndia; she was pretty and very innocent looking and very skilful in abducting and executing Russians; she carried out at least fifteen successful operations; all the victims were Russians.

Tajwar herself was involved in the preparation and dissemination of anti-regime pamphlets and posters as well as the intimidation of members of the administrative staff inclined to collaborate with the regime. A person was warned three times, after the third warning his case was handed over to the operational section.

Usually women obtained information from their connections in the administration and would pass them to urban Resistance groups for their own use and for the use of commanders in the countryside. The majority of cases of Russians and enemy agents who disappeared or were killed were due to the initiative of women. They were also responsible for a majority of the bomb explosions.

But they also suffered heavy losses. Hundreds of women and girls were arrested, tortured and executed. She spent one year in prison (1983) and suffered the most horrible torture (her experience as prisoner will be reported in our series 'Life in Kabul Jails').

She confirmed the information concerning women Resistance in the provincial cities. Apart from the women in Kunduz in the north, whom she organized herself, there are strong female Resistance movements in Herat and Kandahar cities in the west. In Herat, Commander Razia, a lady Resistance fighter, is well known. Her father was a freedom fighter and was killed. Then her brother replaced him as commander and was also killed. Razia took her brother's job and formed in 1983 an independent group of women fighters; they were given arms and are even carrying out operations in the countryside.

Inside Kandahar city women have been increasingly involved in the Resistance since 1981. Old women are given the task of looking after the children and the house. The young ones are freed to work with the muhjahidin. They carry arms, ammunition and information under their veils; the pretty ones attract Russians or Kabul agents and lead them to a house in which the muhjahidin are waiting for them.

Afghan Information Centre
Monthly Bulletin
No 58, January 1986

Life in Afghan Jails
Interview with Tajwar Sultan – Part II

Mrs Tajwar Kakar, known in the resistance as Tajwar Sultan, describing her experience in the underground Resistance movement (see AIC Monthly Bulletin No. 57,

Dec. 1985), also talked about her life in jail. Here is the second part of her interview.

She was arrested for the first time on 26 December, 1982, as she said:

'Some members of my underground cell were arrested and my name was revealed. I was closely watched and followed by the KHAD agents.'

In addition to other activities Mrs Kakar was organizing a demonstration for 27 December (the anniversary of the Soviet invasion). On 26 December at 11.00 a.m. two jeeps full of armed men came to her door and two women entered her house and instructed her to go with them without telling her where or why. She had already given instruction to her daughter Fauzia, sixteen years old, and her son Temor, twelve, that in the case of her arrest, they had to take all the documents hidden in the house to a safer place, and inform her colleagues not to come to the house. She was lucky that when her house was inspected, all the documents had already been removed. First she was led to KHAD headquarters in Shishdarak. She was taken to room number 11 located in the upper storey of the building. The room had no furniture, was cold and humid. They took her coat and sweater away. At 11.00 p.m. she was led to a large room located in the basement. Three groups of people were seated in different corners of the room, including a Russian adviser. Mrs Kakar was ordered to sit on a metal chair with devices for fastening the hands and feet. First her hands and feet were tied to the chair and then interrogation started. Questions, worded differently, were put to her by different people, starting with questions about her identity, her place of residence in Kunduz and close relatives. Then a box of money was placed in front of her. Mrs Kakar was told that if she co-operated, her children would be sent abroad for further education and she would be given the money and released. The Russian adviser, who spoke in Pashtu, said that if she named just one person's connection with her, that would be enough.

Mrs Kakar said:

'I lost my temper and replied that he was a stranger and had no right to ask me what I do in my own country. The men became angry and attacked me. I was hit on my mouth by a heavy fist, and kicked with boots. Some of them started pulling me by the hair from one side to the other. Blood ran out of my mouth, ears, and nose. One of them took a pistol and pointed it at my head and said, "I am going to count from one to fifty; if you have not answered by then, you will be shot." He began counting and the others started questioning. I was asked, "Tell us who are the leaders of your band." I replied that I knew some famous ones: Taraki and Amin. Immediately, from one of the three groups present, someone rushed towards me and started beating me with electric sticks. Every stick gave me an electric shock and horrible pain. I fell unconscious for some time. When I regained my senses I was asked what kind of activity I planned to perform on 27 December. As they did not have any proof, I kept silent. The whole night was spent in beatings and questioning. In the morning they dug a hole in the snow and buried me up to the neck. At first I felt chilled and cold, but after a while I felt numb and did not feel the pain. In the evening I was brought back to a room and given a piece of bread. Before being arrested I had been told that hunger helped one suffer less under torture. Because of this I ate very little. The interrogation continued for seven days. During this time

151

they kept me awake by exposing my eyes to powerful light. On the fourth night of interrogation in the underground room they brought a special device connected to sharp needles. They punched the needles inside my finger nails and pushed a button. It gave me a strong electric shock and the nails started to come apart (the broken nails are still visible on Mrs Kakar's hands). *On the seventh day, as they failed to get any confession, they threatened that my husband and children would be brought in front of me and tortured.'*

From there she was transferred to Sedarat (the prime ministry) and was locked in a room. One night some pain-killing pills were brought to her. She suspected the pills and kept them in a hidden place. Two women, one claiming to be a member of Hezb-e-Islami, and the other identifying herself as a member of Jamiat, came to her room. She suspected them and did not believe what they said. Mrs Kakar gave the pill to one of them who was complaining of a headache. She took it and after a while she relaxed, became cheerful, and revealed her true identity as a KHAD agent, showing her a small tape recorder which she carried under her shirt. After one month of interrogation she was transferred to an ordinary room. The interrogators, including Russians, failed to force her to confess or obtain any proof showing her involvement in the Resistance activities. In Sedarat, Tajwar saw two elderly women: one a seventy-year-old from Panjsher who had been arrested carrying ammunition in a basket of grapes, and the other a sixty-year-old from Baghlan. There was also a whole family in that prison. The men were detained in a separate section; the women and children were jailed with Tajwar and other female prisoners. The family had wanted to flee from East

Germany to the West but had been arrested at the East German border and handed over by the authorities to the Kabul regime. Later, the smaller children were sent to Watan Nursery (a Russian special training centre). There was also an elderly woman under pressure to tape her voice and ask her two young sons to come back from exile in Germany. The two boys were on a wanted list and would have been executed upon their arrival. Therefore, the mother, knowing this, refused to do so.

Mrs Kakar further said that after one month of physical torture, the psychological torture started. Once, they showed her a letter indicating her husband's intention to divorce her on the grounds that she has lost her reputation as a good woman by being in jail. Another time, they told her that her daughter Fauzia had been run over by a car and killed.

She said:

'One day I was taken to a large room. They pointed to a curtain and said that there was my daughter Fauzia, sixteen years' old. They gave me a piece of paper to write my confession. Then I heard sounds of beating, slapping mixed with cries, and shouting. My body became tense, I thought I was going to faint. I had a feeling of sinking in a dark cave where sounds from a distance were heard. I was chilled, shaken and confused. This type of torture continued for a week. I looked for Fauzia among the prisoners. After one month I saw a young girl. I rushed towards her; when she turned her face it was not Fauzia. Her nails were broken and blackened. She was suffering from a nervous breakdown.'

After one year of detention, as they had failed to obtain any documents or confessions, Mrs Kakar was released. She returned home on 3 May, 1982. She was given a job as a teacher in Qala-e-Shada primary school. She went back to Kunduz. There she established contact with some commanders from Jamiat-o-Islami (Prof. Rabani). She carried out her Resistance activities until April 1984, when Farouq Miakhel, who knew all about her, was appointed as KHAD officer in Kunduz. Helped by Resistance friends, she fled the area. She went to Kabul and from there to Ghazni. Muhjahidin helped her to cross the border and join the Afghans in exile.

PART FOUR

*The Strange Case
Of The
Western Conscience*

Coming out of Pakistan it was as if a clamour suddenly fell silent. In Peshawar I was meeting Afghans all the time, refugees and fighters, and each one had a plea, implicit or very explicit indeed: a terrible anguish of need. If I had been able to bring myself to say: 'Every day on the television screens we in the West see suffering, like yours, from several parts of the world,' the reply would certainly have been: 'Yes, but it is we who are fighting for you against a common enemy.' They cannot understand why we do not help them. They are, all the time, surprised at our short-sightedness. They are also reproachful, incredulous, astonished, silent with hurt pride. A few of them have been driven to beg, needing to feed families – but not many, for Afghan pride is strong. Some demand, because they feel aid is their right. They expostulate. They reason with you.

And then, suddenly, the indifference of the West – silence. Even if you have expected it, it is a shock. Painful.

In *The Times* of 22 November was a small piece saying that 60,000 Afghans were fleeing to Pakistan, because the Russians had destroyed crops (they burn them in the fields). As Pakistan is no longer registering refugees for food and aid, many of these 60,000 people will die. Many of the previous outflows of refugees have died – are dying now. This piece of news was on an inside page. Information about Afghanistan is always relegated to that part of a newspaper which is reserved for secondary and unimportant news.

157

It is a good deal that the information is there at all. Two years ago I was in Toronto, and the Wall Street Journal asked to interview me. The young woman who came said she would like me to talk about what interested me. Impressed by this novel approach by a journalist, I said I would like to talk about Afghanistan, which had been fighting the Russians for five years, with little or no assistance from the outside world. Her face showed she was already losing interest. I said it was unprecedented for a war to be fought for five years by a virtually unarmed people against a super power, while the world took virtually no notice. She murmured, at once, 'Vietnam' – as I expected she would. I said that the Vietnamese had been armed, equipped. I said that a million Afghan civilians had been murdered by the Russians. There were five million Afghans in exile – it was as if a third of the population of the United States had taken refuge from an aggressor in Canada. At this she announced that it was all very hard to believe. The interview then continued on all too familiar lines. When it was printed, there was no mention of Afghanistan. Since then, the *Wall Street Journal* has been, as we say, 'very good' about Afghanistan. But anyone involved in this business knows that there is a wall of indifference, both in Britain and in the United States, and this is so strong, so irrational, one has to begin asking why.

There are 'about' ten million refugees in the world, and half of them are Afghan. You never see figures of Afghan refugees as a headline, but very often indeed the headlines, 'So and so many thousand refugees in Sudan/Ethiopia.'

What determines the newsworthiness of a catastrophe? Why has the horror of Afghanistan never been considered

158

important? To answer such questions, it seems to me, would explain a good deal of the assumptions and prejudice that govern our organs of information.

The articles I wrote about what I saw in the refugee camps in Pakistan, about what I heard from the Afghan fighters, have been refused by all the American and European newspapers they were sent to. By the *Washington Post*. By *Time*. By *Newsweek*. By the *New Yorker*. And the *New York Times* magazine section wanted something 'more personal'.

I take the liberty of believing that had these articles been on another topic not subject to this mysterious inhibition, this ukase, they would have been printed.

Just after I returned from Pakistan there was a television programme in the 'Everyman' series. It pictured the muhjahidin as crazed, drugged fanatics, babbling about their rights to a paradisal bliss of fair maidens and beautiful boys (causing some jolly jokes in the press about the homosexual warriors of Afghanistan). Much was made of their ill-treating a man suspected of being a spy. The muhjahidin have never presented themselves as anything else but guerillas fighting by any means at all to free their country: they do not, like the Russians, lie about how they fight. This programme made a bad impression on various people I knew who saw it. 'If that is what the Afghans are like,' said they, 'then it is just as well the Russians are taking them in hand.' This illustrates that reaction characterized by the Afghans as a symptom of our still-imperialist nature: unable ourselves now to 'civilize' backward peoples, we take part, by proxy, in the Russian imperialism. I asked my agent, Mr Jonathan Clowes, to find out if the TV channel in question would permit me to

put another point of view: I had just returned from Pakistan and thought the programme was biased, not to say
offensive. This programme and two others said in effect,
'No, Afghanistan is just a bore.' 'No one is interested in
Afghanistan.' This neatly illustrates the media's way of
sheltering behind attitudes they have themselves created.
Treat a subject as a bore: put it always on an inside page –
and then say there is no interest in it. The fourth programme said it would be prepared to do an interview,
provided that I understood Afghanistan would merely be a
jumping-off ground for more interesting topics: probably
the surprising and novel news that I don't approve of
apartheid, am unhappy (like everyone else) about the
situation in Southern Africa.

The 'Everyman' programme, if it had been fairly doing
its job of informing, should have explained to viewers who
know nothing at all about the Afghan situation – partly
because they have not been told, partly because of a psychological block reinforced by media attitudes – that:

(a) there are seven political parties in Pakistan, all
claiming to represent Afghanistan, all with very different
viewpoints, while all being based on Islam. All will take
film-makers into Afghanistan. When in Peshawar it is a
question of finding a group that will trust you. 'Everyman'
chose, or was chosen by, an extreme group, and it should
have been said that had they gone in with a different
group, a different picture would have emerged.

(b) The muhjahidin don't go to so much trouble, take so
many risks, for the sake of giving western viewers half an
hour's exotic experience. They do it because they need
help, and they believe, poor souls, that if we, the West, see
what they are experiencing, we will want to help. Why was

nothing said about their need? That they are starving? That the Russians destroy crops and irrigation systems? That they are desperate for warm clothes, for food – that they need these things urgently?

How many of the muhjahidin, how many of the people fleeing from the Russians, how many of the people still living inside, will die this winter and spring? I expect to see, tucked away on the back pages of *The Times*, or the *Independent*, or the *Guardian*: 'It is estimated that hundreds of thousands of Afghans have died of starvation in the winter and spring months.' While on the front page are headlines about famine in Africa.

It is hard to get figures for deaths from starvation in Africa. Impressed by that engaging young man Bob Geldof's shout to the world 'Twenty-two million people are starving to the death in Africa', I tried to track down the real figures. According to Peter Gill's book, recommended by Oxfam, *A Year in the Death of Africa*, 200,000 people certainly died of famine in 1984–5. According to expert foreign relief officials, the total figures 'may have' reached a million.

Why are these 200,000 or a million Africans so much more deserving of headlines than the equivalent number of Afghans?

It is because, for some reason or other, we are sensitized to Africa.

A month ago, a friend trying to get contributions for Afghan Relief in Kent was told by a woman that, 'We have our own charities, nearer home, to think about.' Asked if she had contributed to Ethiopian famine relief, she said, 'Of course.'

There are some standard responses to the situation of

161

Afghanistan. It was discouraging coming home, experiencing such a narrow range of push-button responses.

'Afghanistan is the Soviet Union's Vietnam.' Well, when you analyse it, no it isn't, except that in both cases 'undeveloped', (or if you like, 'Third World') people opposed, oppose, powerful world powers. For one thing, the Vietnamese had all kinds of weapons, training, aid. For another, the war was fought in a blaze of publicity, it was a televized war. We watched it progress, on our television screen, night after night.

'Did you know that the Russians have tied living people together, poured petrol over them, and set fire to them?' I asked.

Judiciously: 'Like the Americans in Vietnam.'

'Well, actually, no. They did not.'

'They used napalm, that comes to the same thing.'

'Well, that's all right then, isn't it?' I suppose one could say.

From a nurse in a hospital, who asked where I had been, 'Where's that?'

From another, an Irishwoman, told that half the world's refugees are Afghans: 'The trouble with these people is that they have so many children.'

On the radio, a journalist who had interviewed a fundamentalist guerilla leader and disagreed with certain of his attitudes: 'Why are we supporting such people?' Then, in a light humorous voice: 'I suppose to bash the Russians.'

Listening to the tones of voice people use when discussing Afghanistan is revealing. A light, humorous voice is common: the one always used, deliberately or unconsciously, on the media to signal to listeners or viewers that the matter isn't serious.

162

The radio again: The United Nations Commissioner for Refugees was asking for forty million pounds because the conditions for refugees everywhere was worsening. Two examples were given. The second was that certain work programmes in Pakistan for Afghan refugees were being cut. The commentator was in a hurry to get to something more interesting, and he spoke in a light, casual voice, thrown away . . . you'd never guess we were talking about people who might die without these work programmes.

When I was leaving Pakistan, the Russians were making a big thing of withdrawing a certain number of their troops. Everyone in Pakistan, all the Afghans, knew that this was another clever propaganda move and that the West would fall for it. While experts certainly said it was, analysing why the withdrawal of these troops would not make any difference, people I met all seemed anxious to believe the Russians' claim. 'But they are already withdrawing their troops aren't they?'

Another Russian ploy that the West seemed anxious to accept: they paraded captured muhjahidin, making them say how happy they were to surrender and how much all their fellows longed to surrender too – the same fighters were produced, again and again. This reminded me of a certain Dartmoor sheep farmer who used to entertain us Londoners with accounts of how, when officials came down to count his sheep, each of which earned a government subsidy, he – the farmer – would drive the same sheep around and around and around, three or four times. 'The silly buggers never noticed.'

Currently Gorbachev is claiming that there will be an early end to the Afghan War. This is what appears again and again heading paragraphs in the newspapers. People read AN EARLY END TO THE AFGHAN WAR – and you hear people saying, 'But Gorbachev is ending the war, isn't he?' In fact, things are exactly where they were. Gorbachev wants aid to the guerillas stopped – such as it is – before he agrees to withdraw. He knows, if the readers of the *Guardian, Independent,* etc, do not, that the people actually doing the fighting, the muhjahidin, will not stop fighting on the basis of anything so flimsy as a promise from him. They will not stop fighting even if the slight flow of aid does dry up – they will go on capturing arms from the Russians as they have done from the start. This is a repetition of the end of the war in the old Southern Rhodesia: interminable talks went on at endless conference tables, but the people actually doing the fighting, the guerilla fighters, were not invited. There would be no conferences and discussions over the Afghan war now if the muhjahidin had not gone on fighting, year in, year out, despite the continual announcements by western journalists that they were defeated.

The Gorbachev claim: 'There will be an early end to the Afghan War', is yet another clever ploy by clever propagandists.

Reporting on the negotiations for concluding the Afghan War, a new note is being struck. One of the obstacles – so we are being told – to the Soviet agreement to conclude the war, is its dislike of Islamic Fundamentalism. They do not dislike Fundamentalism. They are working very closely with Khomeini's Iran, supplying arms, experts and advisers, technology, machinery. I heard high-level Afghans describe Iran as a Soviet satellite. But they know that we very much dislike and fear Islamic

Fundamentalism. They are deliberately playing on this dislike, this fear.

Why do we fall for it, again and again? And again.

The reason is deep in our psychology, is rooted in attitudes which are taken for granted, largely unexamined. Unexamined certainly by those in whom they are strongest.

There is a reluctance to criticize the Soviet Union. After all that has happened, all the information we have had about the place, an inhibition persists and is cleverly manipulated by the Russians.

It is almost impossible to raise this subject without being accused of being 'reactionary' – so polarized have our responses become, and I feel a sort of despair even trying. There is a web, or spectrum, of attitudes, highlighted at one end by the court case at this moment going on in Australia, over exactly how much we, the citizens, are going to be told about how many Soviet agents there have been in high places in this country: how much treachery has been going on, to use a quaint old-fashioned term. The other end of the spectrum is precisely this reluctance to criticize the Russians for anything, this readiness to excuse them. So, if the Soviet Union, at Chernobyl, releases radioactivity that poisons its own waters and soil, and will cause the deaths of no one yet knows how many of its citizens, that poisons crops and soil all over Europe, with still unknown long-term results, then in no time at all we will be reading and hearing Chernobyl and Three Mile Island equated – Three Mile Island which killed no one, and did not poison food, animals and soil. It means that if the Soviet Union shoots down a civilian airliner with the loss of everyone aboard, almost at once this will be in some way proved to be the fault of the US, and very soon the incident will be lodged in people's minds as equally the fault of the Soviet Union and the US. It turns out that, in fact, the evidence seems to show that the United States was not at fault. But whether it was or not will make no difference: there is a need to think it is.

The United States' (to my mind, mistaken) policy in Nicaragua is relentlessly criticized at the top of everybody's voice, vituperously, endlessly – but the Soviet policy in Afghanistan is excused, softened.

This complex of attitudes is fascinating the psychologists, and will fascinate the historians even more.

How, they will ask, did it come about that the most brutal, cynical regime of its time, was so much admired, excused, by people describing themselves as humanists, humanitarians, democrats, and long after its true nature was thoroughly exposed?

Perhaps there are hints, suggestions we can study.

For instance: recently, a Russian said on television that a remark from a critic to the effect that the Soviet regime had murdered ten times as many people as Hitler, had been censored out of a programme, 'because it would hurt the feelings of us Russians.' Which must remind people of my generation of a remark made by a certain female Russian party apparatchik who, faced with Khrushchev's speech at the Twentieth Congress, said daintily that she didn't think it ought ever to have been made, because 'it isn't very nice for us, is it?'

Well, no, none of it was very nice for those of us who went along (for whatever length of time it was) with the Soviet 'dream'.

Which murdered so many . . . how many?

166

Oh, these estimates! 'It is estimated that . . .'

Was it *seven million* or *nine million* deliberately murdered during the forcible collectivization of the peasants in the Soviet Union? By Stalin. As it is put: 'Stalin murdered. . .' as if he did it with his own hands alone. But it was with the enthusiastic and efficient co-operation of hundreds of thousands of devoted Communist Party members.

Apparently it was not *twenty million* Russian soldiers who died in the last war, but *eight million* – as Stalin himself said. The *twenty million* now cited (by the West too, following the Russians' lead) includes all those murdered by Stalin (with the enthusiastic and efficient co-operation of Party members) in Gulag.

These figures are themselves in question – not the *eight million* who died in the war (if Stalin is to be believed) but the *twelve million* murdered. According to Victor Suvorov (the pseudonym of a Soviet officer who defected), the Soviet demographers say that the population should have reached 315 million in 1959, but the census showed only 209 million. Where, he asks, are the missing hundred million? (Hitler, he says, is estimated to have 'executed' twenty million.)

What's twenty million? Or even a hundred million, these days?

When I read that, during The Great Leap Forward in China, between twenty and forty million had died, I thought this must be the apotheosis of statistical whimsicality, until a short time later came the news that 'between twenty and eighty million had died during the Cultural Revolution'. (Both campaigns, of course, were conducted with the enthusiastic and skilled co-operation of devoted comrades.) Mind you, this cavalier attitude to the deaths of millions of Chinese probably derives from the Chinese themselves. Mao Tse Tung, addressing a crowd of around a million people in Bei Jing, shouted that it would not matter if the West did drop nuclear weapons on his people and kill half the population because there would be plenty of Chinese left. The crowd, I was told by a friend who was present, roared approval.

Statistics are tricky for other reasons than the *amour propre* of murderers, or the round figures of statisticians. When I told the *Wall Street Journal* woman two years' ago that there were two and a half million refugees in Pakistan, I was scaling it down, because of the enormity of it: the figure was already supposed to be three and a half million.

On this trip we heard various estimates, ranging from three and a half to four and a half million refugees in Pakistan; between half a million and two million in Iran. The wide divergence of figures in Iran seems to me a bad thing: an indication of worse than indifference, perhaps a cover-up.

Exiles from Afghanistan are always visualized as the people in the camps. But in addition there are hundreds of thousands in exile in London, Paris, Canada, the USA, and Australia. These are mostly middle class – the educated members of the population who were not murdered, who are not still in prisons in Afghanistan. These refugees are never mentioned.

In a world where we can accept as normal 'Between twenty and eighty million people were killed . . .' I suppose five million Afghan refugees are hardly worth mentioning. And the million Afghan civilians murdered by the Russians? This figure, it is estimated, is now much higher – is growing larger all the time.

The people murdered by the Khmer Rouge, two million of the population, were not mentioned either. At the time no one demonstrated for them, the humanitarians were not protesting, circulating petitions. But then they were murdered by a communist dictator – (with the energetic co-operation of the young comrades,) so the automatic inhibition came into action: rather bad taste, really, to mention it.

What has happened is that we have been conditioned to see Hitler's Germany, which lasted for thirteen years, a very short time, as the archetype of evil for our time; have accepted this continual hammering on one nerve.

Several times a week we read, or hear, versions of this: 'So and so is the worst butcher since Hitler.' This pattern of thinking ignores Stalin, Mao Tse Tung, Pol Pot, the invaders of Afghanistan.

It has probably often happened in the past that a terrible atrocity has become the symbol or shorthand for other, lesser or greater, atrocities, so that they become forgotten. Our minds seem to work like this. We may observe how they work watching the changes in how we refer to the murder of six million Jews. When the news was fresh, we said, 'the six million Jews murdered in the gas chambers by Hitler.' This became shortened to 'the six million Jews murdered by Hitler.' While our minds cannot really take in the enormity of the six million, at least this is a number, a figure, standing for people, for human beings; but now there is a catch-phrase, The Holocaust, because of a television programme. The humanity of the murdered people is diminished by the slogan. Soon we may forget how many people were killed. We have already forgotten, because of this way we have of making Hitler stand for the evils of our time, the Jews murdered by Stalin who, in the few years just before he died, (referred to then as 'The Black Years') were systematically killed in the newly occupied countries of Eastern Europe and in the Soviet Union itself. It is on record that medieval tortures, medieval methods of killing, were brought out of museums and used. These poor victims are not mentioned now. How many were there of them? Hundreds of thousands? A million? Who knows! Are they ignored because there were comparatively few of them? I don't think there are any memorials to them anywhere.

We consider some forms of murder worse than others. Why should the murder of the six million Jews be worse than, let's say, the deliberate killing, by starvation, as a matter of policy, of seven to nine million, mostly Ukrainian, peasants? If one were to ask this – and it certainly needs temerity to ask – the reply would be, 'Because it was a deliberate, racial murder, qualitatively different, because of the use of the gas chambers.' But this 'six million' – the Holocaust – has itself been simplified. Hitler also killed, on racial grounds, 'about' one million gypsies. Many of them in the gas chambers. They died because they were gypsies, and – Hitler said – racially inferior. These people are never mentioned. There are no books written by the victims, no television or radio programmes, no memorial services, no memorials to the 'approximately' one million gypsies murdered by Hitler. (And, of course, by his party members). Do we share Hitler's view that gypsies do not matter? Of course not: it is just that this enormity has been swallowed by something greater – in number. But if six million Jews are a Holocaust, then are not one million gypsies one sixth of a Holocaust? Should we not put aside this word, Holocaust, and use language that shows some thought, and care, for the dead?

Not only the gypsies have been forgotten. Hitler is supposed to have murdered, in Germany and in the countries occupied by Germany, 'about' twelve million people. Six million Jews, one million gypsies – that makes seven million, and leaves five million. Who were they? Before the murder of the 'racially inferior' Jews and gypsies began, many Germans resisted Hitler and were killed. Hitler's Germany murdered German communists, socialists, trade unionists, and ordinary decent people. The wound made by the killing of the Jews in the extermination camps is so deep that it has been almost impossible to concede any humanity to the Germans of that time. But surely at some point we should start looking at the whole business more coolly? Who were these other five million murdered by Hitler? How many of them were German? Is it not time that the Germans who were the first to fight Hitler (and they must have felt themselves the loneliest, the most isolated people in the world, for no one then was standing up to Hitler) – is it not time they were counted, and honoured, their story at last told? Until we do this I believe we shall be poorer for it, as we are when we allow ourselves black and white judgements, pattern thinking, over-simplification.

We ourselves are the prisoners of these numbers, these figures, the statistics – the millions; and millions upon millions. Is it possible that our careless, our casual, use of these 'millions' is one of the reasons for brutality, for cruelty?

Writing this, I have been haunted by some words of the Russian poet Osip Mandelstam who died in the Gulag:

'and only my own kind will kill me.'

November 1986

171